MUHLENBERG L W9-DBY-717

The European Community

The
European Community

From the Summit Conference at The Hague
to the Europe of the Ten

Federal Republic of Germany

PUBLIC DOCUMENT
Published by the Press and Information Office of the Government of the Federal Republic of Germany

Printed by Wiesbadener Graphische Betriebe GmbH, Wiesbaden
Printed in Germany, 1972

Contents

I. Statements on the Signing of the Treaties of Accession on January 22, 1972

Statement of the Federal Chancellor on the Signing of the Treaties of Accession to the European Communities by the United Kingdom, Ireland, Denmark and Norway on January 22, 1972

Today, the integration of Western Europe has made good progress. The European Community is gaining new members and new possibilities. We welcome the United Kingdom, Ireland, Denmark and Norway to the Community, confident that, where this is still necessary, the peoples will endorse the decision of their Governments.

Despite all difficulties, the Community has followed a consistent road. Since the summit conference at The Hague in December, 1969, considerable progress has been made, and we have helped to achieve it. The mere fact that the Common Market is widened is of great importance. Out of it, in the course of this decade an economic and monetary union is to develop, and it is necessary at the same time to strengthen political co-operation.

The Community of the Ten must also look outwards. It will be judged not least by its capacity to render its contribution towards preserving peace in the world. It is a matter of, on the one hand, a good partnership with the United States; it is a matter of, on the other hand, improved co-operation with the Eastern neighbours; and, thirdly, it is a matter of the development and the markets in Asia, Africa and Latin America.

Many hopes are bound up with the enlargement of the EEC. These hopes must not be disappointed. I believe that Western Europe can become the large-size area that is the most progressive economically and socially.

Interview of the Federal Chancellor on German Television ("Report from Bonn") on January 21, 1972

Question:

Mr. Chancellor, for the EEC it is now a matter of reconciling the interests of ten instead of, as up to now, six. Will this not make it particularly difficult to achieve a better balancing of these interests, above all when one remembers the nocturnal sittings at Brussels with their deliberations on wines, vegetables and now, in addition, Norwegian fish?

Answer:

It will now, purely technically, be somewhat more complicated; that is true. But to achieve a balance among ten is not necessarily more difficult than among six. Nor will there be a lack of additional balancing factors in one area or another. What is true is—and I say this on the strength of my own experiences when I was Foreign Minister—that additional demands will be made on the Council of Ministers and that consideration must be given as to how the work of the Council of Ministers can be made still more effective.

Question:

How can an EEC that has become larger really function politically at all if it does not feel itself an economic and monetary union more potently than it has up to now, at any rate more potently than could be noted during the last monetary crisis?

Answer:

We are on the way. Only last spring the existing Community approved a phased plan for the development towards the economic and monetary union. Then it received a little setback through the international monetary crisis. But the new members are aware of this plan and have associated themselves with it. Then, in spite of all difficulties, it nevertheless in the end played a considerable part in achieving agreement in Washington before Christmas that it was possible for the West Europeans at last to agree among each other and then with the Americans. But it is quite certain as you say: the Common Market must develop in the direction of a monetary union in this decade. Only naturally we always point out, particularly from the German aspect, that we must have a certain parallelism. Proceeding as an entity in the matter of monetary policy also calls for a larger measure of agreement among one another when it is a question of the substance of economic policy.

Question:

Mr. Chancellor, is it possible to develop a European policy at all if the EEC, as the EEC, does not also seek a political arrangement with Eastern Europe?

Answer:

Well, it is already possible to infer something of what will be taking place in this direction from, I would almost have said, the calendar of fixtures. Even in the course of this present year the West European Community will have a summit conference of the Ten, and thus of the Six and the Four. And then there will be a conference—if it no longer possible this year, then next—on, as one says, security and co-operation in Europe, a conference of all European States, including the Soviet Union in the East, including the Americans and the Canadians on the Western side.

And, in addition to that, I would like to say: it can already been seen that the West European Community is already engaged—and this will continue—in achieving a uniform approach to questions of commercial policy on the same lines. We shall have to discuss this with our partners in the East.

I will just mention a problem that is not strictly one of economic policy: protection against threats to the environment, a subject that is nowadays very much under discussion and an object of attention. I look at it like this: there will be a number of tasks about the solution of which the States in Europe, in East and West, can agree—and the neutral States, which are, of course, always needed as well.

And then there will be yet another quality, an intensified degree of co-operation among those who are active in the European Community. And that is how it will be, I believe, in many another area.

Question:

Mr. Chancellor, today, here in Bonn, Foreign Minister Scheel has propagated the French idea of a Minister of Europe seated in Brussels. Is this a project for the German Government that has still to be tackled even in this present legislative term?

Answer:

That is possible. This is one of the projects which now requires further discussion. However, in just over fourteen days I am in Paris for the next consultation with the French Government and fairly soon afterwards in London to continue the talks with the British.

Since I have mentioned Britain, I will refer here quite openly to a difficulty that has absolutely nothing whatever to do with the substance but simply that this is something new for Britain. So far as the appointment of a Minister of Europe is concerned, the British are likely to be somewhat more reserved than others because—and this I understand—they have an interest in as many of their leading men as possible coming personally to Brussels—at any rate in the initial period—in order to make as many bilateral—or if you will—personal contacts as possible.

In this, we others are a step forward and would be able, therefore, sooner to contemplate this new instrument of coordination or harmonization within the individual Governments and then at the Brussels level. But, as I just said, this is one of the propositions about which we shall have to have further discussions with our partners in the existing Community and with the new members.

Statement of the Federal Minister for Foreign Affairs, Walter Scheel, on the "Enlargement of the European Communities—Stocktaking and Perspectives" on January 21, 1972, before the Federal Press Conference in Bonn

I. Tomorrow, in Brussels, the accession of the United Kingdom, Ireland, Denmark and Norway to the European Communities will take place. The EEC's economic potential will be increased by a third. Two hundred and sixty million people will be coexisting and working in one community. The new EEC is by far the largest trading power in the world. With a gross national product in 1970 of 564,000 million dollars, the Ten will be outstripped only by the United States.

The road to the larger Western Europe had its beginning in the hopelessness of the post-war times. Then came the Council of Europe, the European Coal and Steel Community. The Treaties of Rome gave Western Europe a new shape.

After only a few years of rapid development, the process of European integration stagnated from 1963 onwards. It seemed impossible to enlarge the Communities. It was only with the summit conference at The Hague that we set Europe going again and widened the scope of its co-operation. With the Munich conference of November, 1970, political co-operation took its place beside economic co-operation. Already the candidates for accession participated in both events on a status of equality. The success did not come overnight.

We have reached the goal not with perfectionist drawing-board designs but because we made a start where progress was possible: enlargement with a specific balancing of the Member States' interests, internal development of the Communities, and political consultations.

The purpose of the enlargement was to increase the dynamics of the Communities. For this, however, a genuine stocktaking is necessary. We must also realize wrongful developments and redress them in good time. The further development of Europe will not be easier than on the part of the road we have already covered. It is more difficult to balance the interests of ten than the interests of six. Nor can a balancing of interests by itself bring the Community further along the road; what is required are more penetrating impulses dissociated from national interests.

II. It will not be easy to evoke such impulses. In the enlarged Community too there will, for the time being, be no majority decisions. As is well-known, only formally did the Luxembourg Protocol of 1966 take account of this provision of the Treaties of Rome; in this point the actual political aim was never achieved. If there is talk of the degree of integration that has been achieved, of the communal achievements

13

(*acquis communautaire*), then this must not be overlooked. On this, even sweet-sounding action programmes now and again circulating come to grief.

It is therefore necessary to make a start with what has really been achieved and is achievable. This demands a look at the present structure of the Community. An X-ray of this structure shows that it has a good constitution but that there are imperfect formations.

Everybody who has experienced the nocturnal sittings in Brussels knows this. The Council is overtaxed; it takes decisions on individual technical questions below the normal competency of the Ministers, and it frequently takes decisions without the Minitsers being able to be informed adequately on individual technical questions. For example, in the case of the wine regulations we have taken decisions on Oechsle degrees—the number of grammes by which one litre of must is heavier than one litre of water—and, in the case of the enlargement, on problems facing the British farmers. With such material for discussion, the political initiative runs the danger of being stifled.

In the case of the negotiations on enlargement, the Commission has co-operated technically in an outstanding manner. In other areas, however, it is merely an administrative organ. There is lacking an institution that can plan on a long-term basis and is able to foretell what the effects of the decisions of the Council of Ministers will have in the future. In short, one is bogged down in detail; perspectives of development are lacking. There is, finally, no genuine parliamentary control and parliamentary initiative. Although the competencies possessed by the Parliament of Europe have been extended, particularly in budgetary matters, the organs of the Community are not yet directly responsible to the Parliament.

III. Irrespective of this, the enlargement of the Community has worldwide consequences. The course of things takes no notice of the imperfection of the Community.

Permit me to name the three most important examples:

1.   The Community of the Ten accounts for 25 per cent. of America's foreign trade. How, therefore, can the now ensuing change of the customs limits and the preference zones leave the United States unaffected? How can the extension of the European agricultural market be a matter of indifference to a country which in 1970 was already exporting agricultural produce to Europe valued at two thousand million dollars? In short: the links between Western Europe and the United States are up for discussion. Here the Community must speak with one voice. For this, it is not enough from case to case to issue a laboriously negotiated order to an organ of the Community.

2.   In our relationship with Eastern Europe we have the conference on security and co-operation in Europe before us. It is precisely on co-operation that both sides place great expectations. It is, however, a matter of co-operation between countries of different systems. It cannot grow spontaneously, but it is only to be achieved by agreements among States. The tasks of the EEC do not remain unaffected by them. As is well-known, the competency for the conclusion of trade agreements devolves upon the Community as early as January 1, 1973. This alone shows that success in the case of co-operation is to be achieved only if here too the Community speaks with one voice.

3.   The enlargement of the Community will also influence the flow of trade for the rest of the world. Last year's monetary crisis showed that we have to embark on a fresh round of trade talks, a second "Kennedy Round". In view of the Community's growing competency for question of trade, our world trading partners expect from it a uniform attitude.

Added to this comes the fact that, with the exception of the United States and Japan, the most important partners in the world monetary system are associated in the enlarged Community. A lasting solution of the world monetary problems is impossible without the co-operation of the Community as a whole. It is setting about instituting a common monetary policy internally. It must demonstrate this and be responsible for it externally.

IV. What are the consequences resulting in the institutional sphere from this state of affairs? We are still far having a common concept. However, such a concept will have to be worked out at the European security conference in the second half of 1972 at the latest. At the last conference of the European Foreign Ministers, in November, 1971, in Rome, I myself gave certain incentives for this. They related to an institutionalized dialogue with the United States, to the improvement of the political consultations, and to the direct participation of the candidates for accession in the consultations.

Last year, President Pompidou made certain suggestions about a preliminary stage to a "European confederation". Whatever the word chosen for the goal seems to me to be less important. The Federal Chancellor once put forward for consideration whether the expression "West European Union" could not be chosen. What is essential is that the further institutional development is based on the security and the improvement of what has been achieved. The supreme aim must be the ability of the Community to act.

And now what? We are prepared to take up the French idea of Ministers of Europe. They should be resident in Brussels although coming under the Foreign Ministries for internal affairs, and this because, on the one hand, the uniformity of the Member States' foreign policy is thereby preserved (in our case, on account of the particular importance attaching to the close connection between policy towards the East and policy towards the West); on the other hand, so that the development of economic policy and foreign policy in Europe is as closely associated as possible; and, thirdly, because the progressive integration of the Community exerts an influence on relations with Third Countries.

The Ministers of Europe should:

- combine the work of the general Council of Ministers with that of the special Ministers' Councils in order to provide a comprehensive view,
- ensure a continual political dialogue with the Commission and the Parliament of Europe,
- coordinate the development of the economic integration and the political co-operation.

Through the appointment of Ministers of Europe the Council of Ministers would receive a higher status as an organ of the Community. This would warrant the Council of Ministers acting, externally too, more vigorously for the Community than hitherto. The experiences connected with the negotiations on accession have shown that the President of the Council of Ministers, as Community spokesman, can also be an effective instrument in representing the interests of the Community towards the outside. A short period in office is, therefore, an impediment. For this reason consideration should be given to extending his period in office to one year. Irrespective of his national function, he could, as spokesman of the Communities at international conferences—the conference on the security of Europe, say—express an opinion.

Besides the Council of Ministers and its President, the Commission could once more be more fully incorporated in the dynamics of the process of integration. It could assume functions such as those possessed by a planning staff in the national Governments. These include that, on the instruction of the Council of Ministers or on its own initiative, it works out plans and options for the further development and makes projections on the effects in the future of Council decisions. This does not, however, mean that it should neglect its functions as an administrative, controlling and supervisory organ of the Community.

V. All these are suggestions. We shall have to discuss them during the preparations for the European summit conference. However, we do not wish to relapse into institutional perfectionism. The belief that Europe would automatically develop out of perfect institutions to form a single unity has already been proved false.

At least as important as the development of the institutions is that, in a number of spheres in the Community, we take political decisions allowing for an integrated European co-operation.

This primarily holds good for the economic and monetary union. In the meantime the Commission has put forward concrete proposals for setting the economic and monetary union in motion once again. They relate to the harmonization of the monetary policy (narrowing of the band limits, a joint system of foreign currency intervention by the Central Banks, creation of a fund for monetary policy co-operation). We welcome this initiative, but the harmonization of the economic policy must run parallel. This includes the coordination of the market development and budgetary policies, of capital transactions and taxation harmonization. The Council of Ministers should give the signal for the continuation of these operations even at its meeting on January 31.

In addition, the Member States will have to take stock of the technological co-operation and put forward proposals for its further development. Here, the position is not favourable. I am thinking in this connection of EURATOM. Britain's great technological potential, which,

partly for financial reasons, it has been impossible fully to exploit up to now, provides us with a fresh opportunity. We should seize it. The Community's economic ability to compete in the future is closely linked with technological progress.

In the harmonization of foreign policy we want to proceed pragmatically. With the political co-operation, priority should be given to the areas of direct practical significance. I have already mentioned the relations with the United States and the preparation for the conference on security and co-operation in Europe. The relationship of the Community with the Third World is also of significance. After all, the Community grants by far the most development aid, already a quarter more than the United States. Already at the next world conference, in April, in Santiago de Chile, the Community has the opportunity to make a contribution of its own. In the Middle East policy the coordinated attitude of the Community in the United Nations has already led to a Resolution which for the first time was tabled jointly by the members of the Community represented there, the United Kingdom included. In the political co-operation we shall continue systematically to take one step after the other. There is no point in behaving as if the political unity of Europe was already established. We have first to do so.

Finally, I come to security policy. The Community must avoid trenching upon the competencies of the Atlantic Alliance. For the forseeable future nothing can replace NATO as guarantor of the security of the Europeans. The Community has not yet grown together sufficiently to aspire to a uniform defence policy. In all probability this chapter will stand at the end of the political unity. This aspect should not, however, be disregarded in any forward-looking future planning of the Communities.

Statement of the Federal Minister of Economics and Finance, Prof. Dr. Karl Schiller, on the Occasion of the Signing of the Treaties on Accession on January 22, 1972, in Brussels

The signing of the treaty on the accession of the United Kingdom, Denmark, Norway and Ireland to the European Communities is one of the most significant political events of our times. It sets the seal on the success of the year-long, ceaseless efforts of all who regard the Community of the Six as an important, but not in the long run an adequate, foundation for the process of economic and political integration in Western Europe.

The Brussels treaty opens up new prospects to the economy. A market with almost 260 million people, in which persons, goods, services and capital can move freely, is both an opportunity and a challenge. The dynamics of such a market promote competition. They will help to increase productivity and raise the general standard of living. The German economy has well stood the test in the present Community. It will also assimilate the impulses resulting from the enlargement of the Community and make use of the possibilities of development offered it.

However, an enlarged Community also imposes new tasks. Externally, its economic weight will be considerably increased. It needs added solidarity and liberality in order to measure up to the associated worldwide responsibility. Internally, the problems on the road to economic and monetary union should not, and must not, jeopardize this goal. In these tasks lies the challenge to all political and social forces sustaining the Community.

Statement of the Federal Minister of Food, Agriculture and Forestry, Josef Ertl, on the Occasion of the Signing of the EEC Treaties on Accession on January 22, 1972

The signing of the EEC treaties on accession by the United Kingdom, Ireland, Denmark and Norway takes place at a time when the whole world longs to end the still countless international tensions and to prevent the origination of new differences. The agreement of the ten States will, therefore, be welcomed, with particular satisfaction, as fresh evidence of the will to achieve lasting peace and purposeful co-operation in Europe. With the conclusion, reached after arduous negotiations, and which will have noticeable effects for the populations of all countries concerned, the European West has added a new, important rung on the ladder to its political and economic union.

Instead of the present 190 million people, there will be, in future, 250 million in the widened Community. For them, on 95 million hectares of farming land, six million agricultural businesses will produce a large part of the food they require. The degree of self-sufficiency of the enlarged EEC will correspond to something like that of the present Community.

On the strength of their mostly advantageous agricultural structure, the farmers in the new Member Countries—particularly in the United Kingdom—are likely to experience little difficulty in the period of transition. For the exceptional conditions of the Norwegian agriculture an appropriate, exceptional ruling has been agreed. The five years of transition will give sufficient time for adaptation to the new production and marketing conditions.

According to the present experience there will be an even more plentiful supply of food-stuffs of ever-improving quality for the consumers. The channels of trade will be adapted to the changed conditions. Precautions have been taken to make sure that, as far as possible, no economic harm is done to the EFTA countries not seeking entry nor to the non-European countries with a particularly close historical trading link with the United Kingdom.

The Common Market of the Ten is the logical political step which had to follow the co-operation of the existing six countries. It brings nearer to Europe the political, economic and agricultural integration and co-operation which its people need in order to be able to live in peace in a restless world.

II. The Treaty concerning the Accession of Denmark, Ireland, Norway and the United Kingdom to the European Economic Community and the European Atomic Energy Community

TREATY between

the KINGDOM OF BELGIUM,

the FEDERAL REPUBLIC OF GERMANY,

the FRENCH REPUBLIC,

the ITALIAN REPUBLIC,

the GRAND DUCHY OF LUXEMBOURG,

the KINGDOM OF THE NETHERLANDS,

Member States of the Europen Communities,

the KINGDOM OF DENMARK,

IRELAND,

the KINGDOM OF NORWAY,

and the UNITED KINGDOM OF GREAT BRITAIN AND NORTHERN IRELAND

concerning the accession of the Kingdom of Denmark, Ireland, the Kingdom of Norway and the United Kingdom of Great Britain and Northern Ireland to the European Economic Community and to the European Atomic Energy Community.

HIS MAJESTY THE KING OF THE BELGIANS, HER MAJESTY THE QUEEN OF DENMARK, THE PRESIDENT OF THE FEDERAL REPUBLIC OF GERMANY, THE PRESIDENT OF THE FRENCH REPUBLIC, THE PRESIDENT OF IRELAND, THE PRESIDENT OF THE ITALIAN REPUBLIC, HIS ROYAL HIGHNESS THE GRAND DUKE OF LUXEMBOURG, HER MAJESTY THE QUEEN OF THE NETHERLANDS, HIS MAJESTY THE KING OF NORWAY, HER MAJESTY THE QUEEN OF THE UNITED KINGDOM OF GREAT BRITAIN AND NORTHERN IRELAND,

UNITED in their desire to pursue the attainment of the objectives of the Treaty establishing the European Economic Community and the Treaty establishing the European Atomic Energy Community,

DETERMINED in the spirit of those Treaties to construct an ever closer union among the peoples of Europe on the foundations already laid,

CONSIDERING that Article 237 of the Treaty establishing the European Economic Community and Article 205 of the Treaty establishing the European Atomic Energy Community afford European States the opportunity of becoming members of these Communities,

CONSIDERING that the Kingdom of Denmark, Ireland, the Kingdom of Norway and the United Kingdom of Great Britain and Northern Ireland have applied to become members of these Communities,

CONSIDERING that the Council of the European Communities, after having obtained the Opinion of the Commission, has declared itself in favour of the admission of these States,

HAVE DECIDED to establish by common agreement the conditions of admission and the adjustments to be made to the Treaties establishing the European Economic Community and the European Atomic Energy Community, and to this end have designated as their Plenipotentiaries:

HIS MAJESTY THE KING OF THE BELGIANS

Mr G. Eyskens, Prime Minister;
Mr P. Harmel, Minister of Foreign Affairs;
Mr J. van der Meulen, Ambassador,
Permanent Representative to the European Communities;

HER MAJESTY THE QUEEN OF DENMARK

Mr J. O. Krag, Prime Minister;
Mr I. Nørgaard, Minister of External Economic Affairs;
Mr J. Christensen, Secretary General for External Economic Affairs,
Ministry of Foreign Affairs;

THE PRESIDENT OF THE FEDERAL REPUBLIC OF GERMANY

Mr W. Scheel, Minister of Foreign Affairs;
Mr H.-G. Sachs, Ambassador,
Permanent Representative to the European Communities;

THE PRESIDENT OF THE FRENCH REPUBLIC

Mr M. Schuman, Minister of Foreign Affairs;
Mr J.-M. Boegner, Ambassador,
Permanent Representative to the European Communities;

THE PRESIDENT OF IRELAND

Mr J. A. Lynch, Prime Minister;
Mr P. J. Hillery, Minister for Foreign Affairs;

THE PRESIDENT OF THE ITALIAN REPUBLIC

Mr E. Colombo, Prime Minister;
Mr A. Moro, Minister of Foreign Affairs;
Mr G. Bombassei Frascani de Vettor, Ambassador,
Permanent Representative to the European Communities;

HIS ROYAL HIGHNESS THE GRAND DUKE OF LUXEMBOURG

Mr G. Thorn, Minister of Foreign Affairs;
Mr J. Dondelinger, Ambassador,
Permanent Representative to the European Communities;

HER MAJESTY THE QUEEN OF THE NETHERLANDS

Mr W. K. N. Schmelzer, Minister of Foreign Affairs;
Mr T. E. Westerterp, State Secretary, Ministry of Foreign Affairs;
Mr E. M. J. A. Sassen, Ambassador,
Permanent Representative to the European Communities;

HIS MAJESTY THE KING OF NORWAY

Mr T. Bratteli, Prime Minister;
Mr A. Cappelen, Minister of Foreign Affairs;
Mr S. Chr. Sommerfelt, Ambassador Extraordinary and Plenipotentiary;

HER MAJESTY THE QUEEN OF THE UNITED KINGDOM OF GREAT BRITAIN AND NORTHERN IRELAND

The Right Honourable Edward Heath, M.B.E., M.P., Prime Minister,
First Lord of the Treasury, Minister for the Civil Service;

The Right Honourable Sir Alec Douglas-Home, K.T., M.P.,
Her Majesty's Principal Secretary of State for Foreign and Commonwealth Affairs;

The Right Honourable Geoffrey Rippon, Q.C., M.P., Chancellor of the Duchy of Lancaster;

Who, having exchanged their Full Powers found in good and due form, have agreed as follows:

Concerning the accession of the Kingdom of Denmark, Ireland, the Kingdom of Norway and the United Kingdom of Great Britain and Northern Ireland to the European Economic Community and to the European Atomic Energy Community

Article 1

1. The Kingdom of Denmark, Ireland, the Kingdom of Norway and the United Kingdom of Great Britain and Northern Ireland hereby become members of the European Economic Community and of the European Atomic Energy Community and Parties to the Treaties establishing these Communities as amended or supplemented.

2. The conditions of admission and the adjustments to the Treaties establishing the European Economic Community and the European Atomic Energy Community necessitated thereby are set out in the Act annexed to this Treaty. The provisions of that Act concerning the European Economic Community and the European Atomic Energy Community shall form an integral part of this Treaty.

3. The provisions concerning the rights and obligations of the Member States and the powers and jurisdiction of the institutions of the Communities as set out in the Treaties referred to in paragraph 1 shall apply in respect of this Treaty.

Article 2

This Treaty will be ratified by the High Contracting Parties in accordance with their respective constitutional requirements. The instruments of ratification will be deposited with the Government of the Italian Republic by 31 December 1972 at the latest.

This Treaty will enter into force on 1 January 1973, provided that all the instruments of ratification have been deposited before that date and that all the instruments of accession to the European Coal and Steel Community are deposited on that date.

If, however, the States referred to in Article 1 (1) have not all deposited their instruments of ratification and accession in due time, the Treaty shall enter into force for those States which have deposited their instruments. In this case, the Council of the European Communities, acting unanimously, shall decide immediately upon such resulting adjustments as have become indispensable, to Article 3 of this Treaty, and to Articles 14, 16, 17, 19, 20, 23, 129, 142, 143, 155 and 160 of the Act concerning the Conditions of Accession and the Adjustments to the Treaties, to the provisions of Annex I to that Act concerning the composition and functioning of various committees, and to Articles 5 and 8 of the Protocol on the Statute of the European Investment Bank; acting unanimously, it may also declare that those provisions of the aforementioned Act which refer expressly to a State which has not deposited its instruments of ratification and accession have lapsed, or it may adjust them.

Article 3

This Treaty, drawn up in a single original in the Danish, Dutch, English, French, German, Irish, Italian and Norwegian languages, all eight texts being equally authentic, will be deposited in the archives of the Government of the Italian Republic, which will transmit a certified copy to each of the Governments of the other signatory States.

DECISION of the Council of the European Communities of 22 January 1972

concerning the accession of the Kingdom of Denmark, Ireland, the Kingdom of Norway, and the United Kingdom of Great Britain and Northern Ireland to the European Coal and Steel Community

The Council of the European Communities,

Having regard to Article 98 of the Treaty establishing the European Coal and Steel Community,

Whereas the Kingdom of Denmark, Ireland, the Kingdom of Norway and the United Kingdom of Great Britain and Northern Ireland have applied to accede to the European Coal and Steel Community,

Having regard to the Opinion of the Commission,

Whereas the conditions of accession to be determined by the Council have been negotiated with the aforementioned States,

Has decided as follows:

Article 1

1. The Kingdom of Denmark, Ireland, the Kingdom of Norway and the United Kingdom of Great Britain and Northern Ireland may become members of the European Coal and Steel Community by acceding, under the conditions laid down in this Decision, to the Treaty establishing that Community, as amended or supplemented.

2. The conditions of accession and the adjustments to the Treaty establishing the European Coal and Steel Community necessitated thereby are set out in the Act annexed to this Decision. The provisions of that Act concerning the European Coal and Steel Community shall form an integral part of this Decision.

3. The provisions concerning the rights and obligations of the Member States and the powers and jurisdiction of the institutions of the Community as set out in the Treaty referred to in paragraph 1 shall apply in respect of this Decision.

Article 2

The instruments of accession of the Kingdom of Denmark, Ireland, the Kingdom of Norway and the United Kingdom of Great Britain and Northern Ireland to the European Coal and Steel Community will be deposited with the Government of the French Republic on 1 January 1973.

Accession will take effect on 1 January 1973, provided that all the instruments of accession have been deposited on that date and that all the instruments of ratification of the Treaty concerning Accession to the European Economic Community and the European Atomic Energy Community have been deposited before that date.

If, however, the States referred to in the first paragraph of this Article have not all deposited their instruments of accession and ratification in due time, accession shall take effect for the other acceding States. In this case, the Council of the European Communities, acting unanimously, shall decide immediately upon such resulting adjustments as have become indispensable, to Article 3 of this Decision, and Articles 12, 13, 16, 17, 19, 20, 22, 142, 155 and 160 of the Act concerning the Conditions of Accession and the Adjustments to the Treaties; acting unanimously, it may also declare that those provisions of the aforementioned Act which refer expressly to a State which has not deposited its instruments of accession and ratification have lapsed, or it may adjust them.

The Government of the French Republic will transmit a certified copy of the instrument of accession of each acceding State to the Governments of the Member States and of the other acceding States.

Article 3

This Decision, drawn up in the Danish, Dutch, English, French, German, Irish, Italian and Norwegian languages, all eight texts being equally authentic, shall be communicated to the Member States of the European Coal and Steel Community, the Kingdom of Denmark, Ireland, the Kingdom of Norway and the United Kingdom of Great Britain and Northern Ireland.

Done at Brussels, 22 January 1972
For the Council
The President
G. THORN

Structure of the Treaty of Accession

I. The "Treaty on Accession" consists of:

1. The *Treaty* on the accession to the European Economic Community and to the European Atomic Energy Community. It was signed by the ten States concluding the Treaty and lays down in its Preamble and three Articles the motives, the extent, and the entry into force of the accession.

2. The *Decision of the Council of the European Communities* pursuant to Article 98 of the ECSC Treaty on the accession to the European Coal and Steel Community. It too consists of three Articles, based according to those of the Treaty on Accession.

3. The *Act on the Conditions of Accession and the Adaptations of the Treaties*. It holds good as a constituent part of both the Treaty and the Decision. Appended to it are various protocols, annexes, exchanges of letters, and the new compulsory versions (Danish, English, Erse, Norwegian) of the original Treaties (with the exception of the ECSC Treaty, which continues binding in the French version only).

4. A *Final Act*, to which are also appended various joint and unilateral statements (e.g., the statement of the Federal Government on the applicability of the accession to Berlin).

An Agreement between the Community and the States acceding lays down the *consultation procedure for the interim period* until the accession becomes effective on January 1, 1973.

II. The *Act* on the conditions of accession is the actual *core* of the treaty instruments. It consists of five parts:

1. "*Principles*": These lay down the type and extent of the commitments resulting for the States acceding from the *assumption* of the *Community legislation* and the *Community standing*.

2. "*Adaptations of the Treaties*": Through the accession, the amendments to the original Treaties are primiarily required in the institutional sphere (composition and voting method of the organs and committees of the Communities). The other adaptations of the Treaties, e.g., of Articles 131 and 227 of EEC-V, are also laid down.

3. "*Adaptations of the Legal Act of the Organs*": This part lays down the amendments to the extensive so-called consequential legislation that will become necessary through the accession, i.e., to the legislation applicable to the organs of the Communities. In order not to overtax and complicate the Act, this part consists of only two Articles referring to Annexes containing the *permanent* adaptations of the consequential legislation already put in hand or still to be formulated.

4. "*Transitional Measures*": This part contains, under seven headings, the stipulations on the make-up of the period of transition, i.e., of the step-by-step approach of the States acceding to the full application of Community legislation, e.g., in the spheres of free trade (approach to the Common Customs Tariff), agriculture, capital transactions, financial contributions, the Community's foreign relations and its system of associations. An integral part of this section of the Treaty is also to be found in the annex containing the *provisional adaptations* of the consequential legislation.

5. "*Stipulations on the Implementation of this Act*": In this part, first of all the transition from the Community of the Six to that of the Ten is laid down, i.e., of the transition to the enlarged organs and committees and the applicability of the consequential legislation.—The final stipulations envisage the transmission of the original Treaties and the attachment of the new linguistic versions to the Treaty on Accession.

III. Synopsis of the Most Important Provisions of the Treaty of Accession, Supplementing Agreements and Protocols

Two basic rules governed the approach to the negotiations: candidate countries were required to accept the Treaties and consequential legislation adopted under the Treaties; necessary adaptations were to be undertaken in the course of a transitional period uniform in time, sector and new Member Country. These were the central principles of the Community's declaration delivered at the inaugural Ministerial Meeting with the negotiating partners in Luxembourg on June 30, 1970. Negotiation on the basis of these principles resulted in the establishment of a general five-year transitional framework at the end of which period the bulk of adaptation would be complete, with the enlarged Community running normally. Certain limited exceptions and amendments to these rules were ultimately negotiated.

One now sees that these basic principles were entirely respected with the exception of a few limited cases. The problems of adaptation were solved by laying down transitional arrangements and not by modifying the existing rules governing the life of the Communities.

I. Transitional Arrangements

The essential context of these transitional arrangements is as follows:

1. *Industry:* A five-year period for complete abolition of tariff and non-tariff barriers between old and new Member States and establishment of a Common External Tariff and commercial policy. Tariffs between Member States will be reduced in five equal steps of 20%, the first to take effect on April 1, 1973, the last on July 1, 1977; the three intermediary cuts to be made on July 1 of each year 1974, 1975, 1976. Adoption of the Common External Tariff by the new members will proceed in four stages:

40%	on January 1, 1974
20% each on	January 1, 1975
	January 1, 1976
and, finally,	July 1, 1977.

Tariff quotas will be introduced on thirteen products *.

2. *Agriculture:* At the very outset of the five-year transitional period new members will adopt all the market organization rules, thus instituting Community preference at the outset. Where, however, specific concrete measures are required for trading reasons, these will be adopted in the terms of Arts. 39 and 110 of the Treaty with due concern for the situation and in conformity with the principles and mechanisms of a common agricultural policy.

The following principles govern the transitional period in agriculture. For products subject to market organization with intervention prices, levies and restitutions, price alignment will proceed in six steps, subject to a flexibility clause up to 10% of the particular alignment to be made. The various penultimate step of alignment will take place for the various products at the beginning of the 1977 marketing year and the final alignment for all products will take place on December 31, 1977.

Intervention prices for each new member will be fixed as a function of that member's price level differences at each stage of price alignment. Levies and restitutions towards Third Countries will equally be fixed as according to these price level differences.

For farm products not subject to intervention price levies and restitutions, customs duties between old and new members will be

---

* The products are: tea, aluminium, silicon carbide, ferro-chrome, ferro-silicon, wood pulp, newsprint, lead, zinc, wattle extract, phosphorous, ply-wood, and alumina.

reduced by one fifth at the beginning of each marketing year when according to the same schedule new Member States will align themselves to the Common External Tariff.

A special timetable was adopted for horti-culture—five equal steps of 20% on December 31 each year from 1973 to 1977. From December 31, 1974, a flexibility clause may be applied of up to 10% of the particular alignment to be made.

II. The Institutional Arrangements

The Institutions of the enlarged Community will be:

I. The *Council* of 10 members, one from each Member State. Voting rights per country will be: Germany 10, France 10, Italy 10, the United Kingdom 10, Belgium 5, the Netherlands 5, Denmark 3, Norway 3, Ireland 3 and Luxembourg 2.

A *qualified majority* applicable when a decision is taken on a Commission proposal will require a minimum of 43 votes. Where the Council decides without a Commission proposal, the 43 necessary votes must represent at least six countries.

A *simple majority* is obtained by 6 out of the 10 Member States.

As for Council Voting Methods within the ECSC Treaty it is not necessary to modify the provisions concerning unanimity, but the majority of 5/6 foreseen in Article 95 (concerning "*la petite révision*") will be increased to 9/10 of Council members.

Where the ECSC Treaty requires a confirmative opinion from the Council, the opinion is considered carried if the proposal of the High Authority gains the agreement of:

- the absolute majority of the Member States including the votes of two of them representing each at least one eighth of the total value of Community coal and steel production,

- or, if the voting is equally split and the High Authority maintains its proposal after a second deliberation, the vote of three Member States representing each at least one eighth of the total value of Community coal and steel production.

Other Council decisions are taken by simple majority including two Member States representing each at least one eighth of the total value of Community coal and steel production.

Rotation of the office of President of the Council will be in alphabetical order of Member States as expressed in their respective languages (Belgique-België, Danmark, Deutschland, France, Ireland, Italia, Luxembourg, Nederland, Norge and United Kingdom). Their order of presidency will operate, as from January 1, 1973, with Belgium in the Chair.

II. The *Commission* will have 14 members, two each from Italy, France, Germany and the United Kingdom and one each from the remaining six countries. The Commission will have 5 Vice-Presidents. Commissioners will hold office for 4 years, the President and Vice-Presidents being appointed for 2 years.

III. *The European Parliament* will have 208 members, the breakdown by nationality being: Italy, France, Germany and the United Kingdom 36 members each, Belgium and the Netherlands 14 each, Denmark, Ireland and Norway 10 and Luxembourg 6.

IV. The *Economic and Social Committee* will have 155 members, 24 each from Germany, France, Italy and the United Kingdom, 12 each from Belgium and the Netherlands, 9 from Ireland, Norway and Denmark and 6 from Luxembourg.

V. The *Court of Justice* will be composed of 11 judges and 3 advocates general. They are appointed for 6 years. Every three years there is a partial renewal affecting alternately 5 judges and 2 advocates general, and 6 judges and one advocate general. For the quorum the presence of 7 judges is required when the court is sitting in plenary session.

VI. The *European Investment Bank* will be composed of a *Council of Governors* to comprise 10 members, one from each Member Country. *Administrative Council* to comprise 19 administrators and 10 substitutes. National representation concerning candidate countries will be:

The United Kingdom: 3 administrators, 2 substitutes

Ireland, Norway and Denmark: 1 administrator each.

Management Committee to comprise 5 members: 1 president and 4 vice-presidents. The number of vice-presidents may be subsequently increased following a unanimous decision of the Council of Governors.

VII. Among *other institutional arrangements* the number of members on the ECSC Consultative Committee will be increased to between 60 and 84. The number of members on the EURATOM Scientific and Technical Committee will be increased to between 20 and 28, the United Kingdom being represented by five members and Denmark, Ireland and Norway by one member each.

VIII. During *the intermediary period* between the close of negotiations and accession to the Rome Treaty, the Community institutions will take into consideration the interest of candidate countries in all proceedings and major policy decisions owing to their position as future members of the Community. This procedure entered into force on November 10, 1971.

(a) At Council level, consultations will take place prior to the adoption of any decisions. This procedure will also apply to decisions taken by applicant countries which might effect their situation as future members of the Community. Such consultations will take place at meetings of an intermediary committee comprising representatives of both the Communities and applicant countries. Community representatives will be members of the Committee of Permanent Representatives or their assistants. The Commission will also be represented. Consultations will normally take place when preparatory work on any given Community project is sufficiently advanced for consultations to be of value. In the case of consultations meeting with serious difficulty, the question may be discussed at Ministerial level at the request of a candidate country.

(b) *The Commission* will make known all its proposals and communications to the candidate countries, after having transmitted them to the Council. In order to ensure that all Commission decisions have taken due consideration of the interests of candidate countries, the Commission will consult these countries before taking any decision that is likely to affect them as future members.

III. The Financial Arrangements

1. The Community Budget

From January 1, 1973, the new Member States will contribute to the Community budget to which they will pay their receipts from agricultural levies and customs duty as well as a proportion of VAT revenue. During the five-year transitional period, however, total contributions from the new Member States will be subject to limitations expressed as percentages of the total Community budget, which will be:

	1973	1974	1975	1976	1977
Denmark	1.099	1.382	1.698	2.040	2.408
Ireland	0.272	0.342	0.421	0.505	0.596
Norway	0.754	0.947	1.164	1.398	1.650
United Kingdom	8.640	10.850	13.340	16.020	18.920

From January 1, 1978, the new Member States will make full contributions, subject to the following conditions:

- in 1978, the increase in contributions from the new members may not total more than 2/5 of the difference between their respective contributions in 1977 and what would have been their full contributions for 1977 had they not benefited from reduced payments during the transitional period.

- in 1979, the increases in the contributions from candidate countries (expressed as a percentage of the Community budget) may not exceed those of the previous year.

Up to January 1, 1978, that part of the new members' normal contributions to the Community budget which is not in fact paid by them because of the transitional period limitations will be divided between the six original members of the Community. This also applies if and when the special conditions for 1978 and 1979 apply.

2. European Investment Bank

New Member Countries will contribute to the capital, statutory reserves and funds of the European Investment Bank according to the following percentage key: Denmark 4%, Ireland 1%, Norway 3%, United Kingdom 30%. In units of account their respective shares of the Bank's capital will amount to: Denmark 60 million, Ireland 15 million, Norway 45 million, United Kingdom 450 million. 20% of these sums will be paid in national currencies within two months of membership, the remainder to be covered by treasury bonds.

IV. Economic and Monetary Affairs

The United Kingdom declared during the course of the negotiations her readiness for an ordered and gradual reduction of sterling balances after membership. In addition, the enlarged Community will discuss appropriate measures for bringing about a progressive alignment of sterling's external characteristics and practices with those of other Community currencies in the framework of progress towards economic and monetary union. Meanwhile the United Kingdom will pursue a policy aimed at stabilizing official sterling balances in a manner compatible with the long-term objectives of economic and monetary union.

In the field of *capital movements* consultations will be held between new members and the Commission on applying measures for liberalization and easing of restrictions. During the first two years of membership new members will remove a series of restrictions notably in the fields of direct investments and individual capital movements. For other capital movements the new members will have up to 5 years in which to effect liberalization.

V. European Coal and Steel Community

Accession to the European Coal and Steel Community takes place pursuant to Article 98 of the ECSC Treaty. The Treaty on Accession contains specific provisions concerning only three points not already covered by the ECSC Treaty and ECSC secondary legislation.

The customs union for coal and steel, as for other products, is to be established by phasing-out internal duties over a period of $4^1/_2$ years; external duties are to be aligned at the same rate. Exports of scrap from the enlarged Community to Third Countries will be permitted only exceptionally and subject to quantitative restrictions. The new Member Countries' export controls vis-à-vis the present Community countries must be dismantled, a process for which Britain is to be allowed two years, Denmark and Norway three and Ireland five.

Under the ECSC Treaty's competition rules, undertakings are required to observe with special care the prohibition on cartels (Article 65). All cartels will have to be notified to the Commission within three months; they may remain in being until the Commission issues a ruling.

Over the years the ECSC has accumulated substantial funds of its own, which it devotes principally to research and social aid. The acceding countries will pay a fixed amount into this fund.

VI. EURATOM

On their accession to the European Atomic Energy Community, new members will adhere to the EURATOM Treaty and the regulations and directives adopted under the Treaty. This implies notably:

1. Common Research Programmes and complementary schemes, as specified by Article 7 of the EURATOM Treaty.
2. A system of safeguard and verification in accordance with both the EURATOM Treaty and the agreement to negotiate between EURATOM and the International Atomic Energy Agency.

The abolition of customs duties within the enlarged Community, and the tariff alignment measures for products in lists A 1 and A 2, will take place at the end of 1973. For products on list B, tariff removal and alignment will be conducted according to the general timetable for industrial goods.

Any propositions for amendment of Chapter 4 of the EURATOM Treaty will be communicated to candidate countries before they are adopted.

Following exploratory conversations, agreement was reached concerning details of information to be exchanged between new and old Member Countries upon accession to the EURATOM Treaty.

VII. Arrangements Concerning the Commonwealth and Dependent Territories

The status quo will be maintained in Britain's trade relations with developing countries of the Commonwealth until December 31, 1975. Meanwhile there will be opportunity to explore and implement new relations between these countries and the enlarged Community according to the following options:

Independent Developing Countries of the Commonwealth in Africa[1], the Indian Ocean[2], the Pacific Ocean[3] and the Caribbean[4] will be given the opportunity to decide on the specific type of agreement they make with the Community, within the following frameworks:

1. Participation in the same Association Agreement as the Community's present Association of African States and Madagascar.
2. Agreement or Individual Agreements with particular emphasis on reciprocal rights and obligations, notably in the trade field.
3. Commercial Agreements with a view to promoting and developing trade between the Communities and the countries concerned.

For Independent Developing Commonwealth Countries in Asia (India, Ceylon, Pakistan, Singapore and Malaysia) the enlarged Community will be ready to examine any problems within the commercial field that may arise in these countries, and in any others within the same region, with a view to finding appropriate solutions. Consideration will be taken of the extent of the Generalized Preferences System.

Dependent Territories[5] of Britain and Norway will be associated with the Communities in accordance with the Part IV of the EEC Treaty. However, the status of the one European Dependent Territory—Gibraltar—will be governed by Article 237, Paragraph 4 of the EEC Treaty, thereby excluding it from any customs arrangements. Thus, the Community customs regulations will not apply to Gibraltar, and all imports from Gibraltar to the EEC will be subjected to the Common Tariff.

The Rome and Paris Treaties will not be applicable to Hong Kong, which will come under the system of Generalized Preferences.

VIII. Other Arrangements

In the course of the negotiations it was agreed that in certain fields or for particular items of the new Member States' legislation or practice special transitional arrangements would be required. The principal matters concerned are set out here below:

1. Sugar

Within the framework of the Commonwealth Sugar Agreement the United Kingdom may continue to import until December 31, 1974, the quantities of sugar at prices previously negotiated in the Agreement.

---

[1] Botswana, Gambia, Ghana, Kenya, Lesotho, Malawi, Nigeria, Sierra Leone, Swaziland, Tanzania, Uganda and Zambia.
[2] Mauritius.
[3] Fiji, Tonga and West Samoa.
[4] Barbados, Guyana, Jamaica, Trinidad and Tobago.

[5] Bahamas, Bermuda, British Honduras, the British Indian Ocean Territory, the Solomon Isles Protectorate, the British Virgin Isles, Brunei, the Cayman Islands, the Falkland Islands and Dependencies, the Seychelles, the Turks and Caicos Islands, Antigua, Dominica, Grenada, St. Lucia, St. Vincent, St. Kitts, Nevis and Anguilla, Norwegian concession territories in the Antarctic.

After this date, the Communities will have as their firm purpose to safeguard the interests of these countries whose economy is largely dependent on the export of basic commodities, and notably sugar. Countries coming into this category are the Independent Developing States of the Commonwealth in the Indian and Pacific Oceans, the Caribbean and the Association of African States and Madagascar. Specific Arran gements will be within the scope of the respective Arrangements with these countries.

The question of Indian sugar exports will be settled in the light of the Communities' Declaration of Intent concerning Independent Members of the Commonwealth in Asia.

2. New Zealand Butter and Cheese

Derogatory quantitive measures in favour of New Zealand dairy products are foreseen in the framework of British adoption of Common Market organization. The timetable for reducing the quantitative guarantees applicable only to the United Kingdom market is fixed for the first five years. Thus, in 1977, the quantitive guarantee for butter will be at 80% of its original level, and 20% for cheese, after which time no further guarantee is anticipated for cheese.

During the course of 1975, the institutions of the enlarged Community will re-examine the question of butter in the light of supply and demand in the principal world producers and consumers, especially in New Zealand and the Community. In the light of this examination, the Council, upon Commission proposal, will rule on appropriate measures for maintaining a derogatory status for New Zealand beyond December 31, 1977.

Finally, the enlarged Community will do its utmost to promote and encourage an International Agreement on Milk Production, in order to improve as soon as possible the world market conditions.

3. Fisheries

By derogation from the Community regulation governing access to fishing waters, Member States of the enlarged Community may limit fishing in their national waters until December 31, 1982, within a six-mile zone to vessels traditionally fishing in these waters from local ports. Special fishing rights enjoyed by Member States in each others' waters, as established from January 31, 1971, are not affected. For specified zones*, fishing limits are extended to 12 miles.

At the latest 6 years from the entry into force of the enlargement Treaty, the Council, on proposal from the Commission, will pronounce on fishing conditions with a view to protecting the sea bed and conserving resources. By December 31, 1982, the Commission will report to the Council on the economic and social development of the coastal regions and the state of marine stocks. On the basis of this report and of the objectives of the Common Fisheries Policy, the Council, upon Commission proposals, will examine the arrangements which could follow the derogations in force until December 31, 1982.

In the case of Norway a protocol was adopted recommending the enlarged Community's institutions to take particular account, during the examination of the Commission's report to the Council, of Norway's fishing problems both from the point of view of Nor-

* Areas subject to the 12-mile rule are: Denmark—the Faroes, Greenland, and the west coasts of Denmark from Tybörön to Blåvandshut. *France*—the departments of Manche, Ile et Vilaine, Côtes du Nord, Finistère and Morbihan. *Ireland*—north and east coasts from Lough Foyle to Cork in the south-west; the east coast from Carlingford Lough to Carnsore Point for shellfish. *Norway*—the west coast from the frontier with the Soviet Union to Egersund. *United Kingdom*—Orkney and Shetland, north and east Scotland from Cape Wrath to Berwick, north-east England from the river Coquet to Flamborough Head, south-west England from Lyme Regis to Hartland Point (including Lundy island), and County Down.

way's economy in general and the special demographic and social structure of the country, so that any subsequent dispositions are undertaken accordingly. Among other measures, these dispositions may include prolongation of the system of derogations beyond December 31, 1982, to the degree necessary and according to rules to be laid down.

4. Norwegian Agriculture

A protocol has been adopted recognizing that the transitional period might prove inadequate to the solution of those particular problems which the Norwegian farmer would come up against because of his country's membership of the Community. It has, therefore, been necessary to foresee specific arrangements which cannot be considered as precedents and which aim at upholding the standards of living of the Norwegian farmers whilst respecting the rules of the Common Agricultural Policy.

Miscellaneous

Among other particular arrangements drawn up during the negotiations, we may note briefly the following. Progress of the *Anglo-Irish Trade Agreement* was deemed compatible with general transitional arrangements on condition that quota arrangements do not disfavour other Community members. On *Ireland's economic and regional development* specific mention will be made in the enlargement Treaty of the Community's intention to act positively to promote expansion of the economy and of living standards. Special measures were also adopted for the *Irish automobile assembly industry* the special production and trading circumstances of which may continue with adjustments until January 1, 1985. *Norway's special pharmaceutical products* arrangements and *trade in alcoholic drinks* were also subject to special dispensations during the transitional period. Special attention was also paid to problems of *veterinary legislation* and satisfactory solutions were found.

IV. Political Statements and Documents from The Hague up to the Accession

Excerpt from the Government Policy Statement of October 28, 1969

Special importance attaches to the forthcoming conference of the Six in The Hague. It may well decide on whether Europe will be taking a courageous step forward with respect to the interrelated subjects of the Community's internal development, intensification and enlargement or whether it will get into a dangerous crisis. The peoples of Europe are waiting for and urging the statesmen to supplement the logic of history by the determination for success.

Franco-German accord may be decisive in this respect. The Federal Government is prepared to lend the close contractual ties that steadfastness which should serve as a model of the type of relations which can today be established between European partners.

The enlargement of the European Community must come. The Community needs the United Kingdom as much as the other applicant countries. In the chorus of European voices the voice of Britain must be not missing, unless Europe wants to inflict harm on itself. We are gratified to note that the decisive forces in British policy continue to be convinced that the United Kingdom in turn needs Europe. It is time to initiate the no doubt difficult and probably time-consuming process at the end of which the Community will find itself placed on a broader basis.

The Federal Government will promote the development of a closer political co-operation in Europe with the aim of evolving step by step a common attitude in international questions. We know that in this endeavour we are in particular agreement with Italy and the Benelux countries.

Statement of the Federal Chancellor at the European Economic Community Summit Conference at The Hague on December 1, 1969

I. If things in Europe were good, we should not be meeting here today. If our Community had already to speak with one voice, then our main theme would be foreign policy: the question of a European peace order, the negotiations with the States of Eastern Europe, our interests in the light of the conflict in the Middle East.

Instead, the success or failure of our conference will rightly be seen in whether or not we bring the European Community ship once more into navigable channels. Concentrated on our narrower problems, we shall not be able to avoid the necessary decisions so that our fellow-countrymen again understand that Europe is more than a matter of market regulations. And so that the young people realize that Europe is more than a recollection of a shadowy, glorious past.

In this connection we are certainly at one in thinking that our Community is to be no *new bloc but an exemplary system* serving as an element of a balanced, all-European peace order. On these lines the Federal Republic of Germany is seeking *understanding with the East in conjunction and harmonization with her partners in the West.*

The association into which we have jointly entered is to be indissoluble and become ever closer. If we wish to achieve the necessary harmonization, we must support one another, i.e., we must cultivate solidarity in practice. I say on behalf of the German Federal Government that we are prepared for this. This readiness is upheld by the approval of our public opinion.

But our people naturally also wish to know what consequences result for them from the European commitments. The German Government, like all others, must also be able to prove that the efforts required of them are meaningful, appropriate and envisionable and that the road we have taken with the West is the right one politically.

Here we are not sitting in the place of the established communal institutions. Here it is more than a matter of an elevated form of the necessary Brussels routine.

II. For this reason I say quite frankly: the German Bundestag and the people of my country expect that I do not return from this conference without concrete arrangements in the matter of the enlargement of the Community.

This matter has been concerning us for years. By virtue of the Treaty it belongs to the basic questions of our Community, and nowhere is it written that we should address ourselves to this only after the period of transition. The German attitude has been well-known for years. I believe that we should no longer shelve this theme.

In the first place, experience has shown that the postponement of the enlargement threatens to paralyze the Community.

Secondly, it is in our common interests if the Community is enlarged at a time in which we are striving for a closer relationship between West and East.

Thirdly, the Community must develop beyond the group of the Six if it wishes to maintain its ground economically and technologically against the giants and discharge its international political responsibility.

I do not hesitate to add a fourth argument: anyone who fears that the economic weight of the Federal Republic of Germany could disturb the equilibrium inside the Community should, also because of this, support the enlargement.

At any rate I say: without the United Kingdom and the other States which are prepared to accede, Europe cannot become what it ought to be and what it can be.

On the strength of the discussions that preceded this conference, I have the impression that we are in fundamental agreement on the enlargement, and this is something not to be under-estimated. Here I would like to address myself to the French President in particular: if today France responds to our clear will to complete and develop the Community with the confidence needed for the enlargement, then that is a cause for satisfaction and acclamation.

Over and above what is fundamental, we are agreed that the States willing to accede to the Treaties would have to accept the aims of the Treaties and the jointly created consequential legislation.

We are also unanimous that the guidelines for the further development, for agreement by us, should be submitted to the candidates for accession. After these guidelines have been made concrete in Resolutions in legal form, they too would have to be submitted to the candidates for accession. Such a procedure would allow—and I am certain of this—development and negotiations on entry to run parallel, so that neither of the two processes holds up the other but that they support each other to the greatest possible extent.

With this, the initial positions for the negotiations are so far prepared that no obstacles stand in the way of their final establishment within a short space of time. I therefore propose that the countries willing to accede be informed that we consider it possible to make a start with the negotiations in the spring of 1970.

We ought to compose the Resolutions on adaptation and transitional wishes of the candidates for accession that are necessary for the conduct of our negotiations during the negotiation itself and present them to the partners as the position of the Community.

Frequently there is talk only of the United Kingdom. This must not be taken to mean that the other countries willing to accede are being neglected.

III. The European interest also demands that there is no disregarding of the future relations with the other members of EFTA. In this connection I am thinking not least of Austria and

Switzerland, because of the situation of my country. Sweden remains, as is well-known, a still open question which in the end only she herself—in close contact with the other Scandinavian countries—can answer.

The close economic involvement of the uncommitted countries with the Community, the free trade realized within EFTA, but also the political function of these countries in the European State system, make it necessary to find a comprehensive economic solution which embraces them. A Community which continues resolutely to follow its economic build-up and political aims can also represent externally such a solution as is necessary in the all-European interest. That the Community takes special situations into account through special measures does not alter its peculiar essence. It does not itself become a preference zone; it remains a Community.

The Federal Government believes that the States here concerned should make their wishes known in good time and be informed about the possibilities of their being met. I suggest a round of talks about this with the candidates for accession and those interested in other forms of co-operation. This should take place as soon as possible after the opening of the negotiations on entry.

IV. Even if here we shall be dealing, in the main, with other tasks, I consider it desirable that we should decide on making a fresh start with the foreign political co-operation. This would have to mean more than merely resuming and continuing the exchange of views within the WEU.

Former differences of opinion about the group of people participating in a qualified foreign political co-operation would be resolved if we were to combine the enlargement of the Community and the political co-operation into a single perspective. We should also, in the wider circle, confirm the "*finalité politique*" of the Community without having to cover the spheres of economic integration and political co-operation.

I suggest that we entrust the Foreign Ministers with working out the draft of an agreement for a gradual development of the political co-operation among our Community's Member States and on the hypothesis that it is to be enlarged.

At the moment it would be a matter of harmonizing well among ourselves our attitude towards the complex of themes of an all-European conference. I hope that in the next few days our representatives in the NATO Council will make a considerable contribution towards finding a constructive solution. No one should have to doubt our wish—after careful preparation, and with the participation of our American allies—to co-operate in finding solutions leading to greater security with fewer armaments and making more practical co-operation between East and West possible.

V. The progressive integration of the six national economies has also entailed a growing dependence in the overall economic development of our countries. Today, economic imbalances between them have a direct effect, and without lengthy hesitation, on the overall development of the Community. Inflationary tendencies in one country rapidly threaten the stability in the others and also the equilibrium within the Community. This leads to distortions and restrictions in the goods, foreign trade and capital transactions; the Community's agricultural market is endangered. Through this development the Community as a whole can suffer. This danger can be averted only if we make more rapid progress on the road to a Community of growth and stability.

My Government is willing to embark on the road to economic and monetary union, however modestly and realistically, step by step. Structural differences between our countries and still existing divergencies in the economic policy aims and ways of behaviour are realities which can be changed only through persistent and common efforts. For this, a convergent behaviour of the large social groups is also needed.

With the harmonization of the aims, a first stage must include an effective coordination of the short-term economic policy. In this, the fixing of medium-term economic policy aims concerning quantities is an important task. If we succeed in developing a common economic policy, we shall be able to realize the economic and monetary union in the second stage.

Such a development will make it necessary to create a European Reserve Fund. For this too I offer the full co-operation of the German Federal Government. As soon as the necessary preconditions have been created, we shall co-operate in the establishment of the European Investment Fund and in deciding its modalities. Then we shall be ready to transfer a certain part of our currency reserves to such a fund for joint administration together with corresponding shares of the reserves our partners would deposit in the Fund.

The Federal Government has not hitherto been found wanting in the readiness to achieve solidarity in economic policy. We hope that the Council's relevant Resolutions can receive concrete form even this present month if possible.

We ought, moreover, to try to set ourselves a time limit for the establishment of the economic and monetary union on the lines of a stable community open to the world. I suggest that the Council takes up this important question and is asked to work out in detail, in close co-operation with the Commission, the stages of such a plan and to approve this phased plan in the course of 1970.

If we decide upon this, we are giving clear evidence of our united will. Let us make a purposeful beginning.

VI. The task in which our countries will have to co-operate in the spheres of economic and technological policies is realized; already, much has been talked and written about it. However, the conclusions from this realization have only slowly been drawn. Before the Community lie some sensible proposals. They have, however, to be embedded within a coherent European technology policy. This calls for political decisions.

This applies particularly to EURATOM. It would not—and I say this quite openly—be acceptable, and not be in accordance with the spirit of our co-operation, if we talked about completion, development and enlargement and at the same time allowed EURATOM's Joint Research Centre, established at great expense, to be at risk, and this because we cannot agree on the utilization and raising of funds which seem small when considered against the overall picture of the Community's projected financing.

It seems to me that with the existing method we are not making progress rapidly enough, with greater unanimity and in much greater detail, and in the nuclear sector more restricted programmes. We cannot here deal with the details of the research programme, but we can—and this I would like to suggest—proclaim our common will to overcome the EURATOM crisis. We should agree to guarantee the existence of the Joint Research Centre, to extend its activity to non-nuclear areas, and to frame its structure and working method with more flexibility.

VII. If there is talk of the build-up of the Community, I must also say a word about the institutions. We are dependent upon their functioning in accordance with the Treaty. This will not show itself until the phase of enlargement.

I propose that
- the Council's working method should be tightened,
- the executive tasks of the Commission should be developed in a pertinent manner,
- the authorities of the Parliament of Europe should be extended, above all by budgetary control.

The structure of the Community must be brought into harmony with the principles of Parliamentary control. Nor, in this connection, must the principle of direct election, laid down in the Treaty, be disregarded.

VIII. The Treaty has laid down that the Community enters into the final phase on January 1, 1970. Our Governments have come to an agreement in the Council to proceed on the hypothesis that the transitional period will not be extended. Consequently, we must do everything in our power to implement the necessary Resolutions.

In the Council it has been seen that not everything that ought to be accomplished by the end of the transitional period can be completed by the end of the year. This also includes subjects in which Germany is greatly interested, such as certain measures for taxation harmonization, trading policy measures, and measures for the removal of restrictions remaining in the domestic market. We are relying on the readiness, proclaimed on all sides, to solve the questions still open as quickly as possible, and desist from calling for solutions by the end of the year.

The actual difficulties lie, as we all know, in the sphere of agricultural financing. For the Federal Government this difficult problem has a fundamental and a practical side.

We support the principle of European solidarity, which must also apply in the course of the build-up and enlargement of our Community. The method and extent of the financing will be determined by the framing of the foreign policy, and its functioning is unsatisfactory for two reasons:

In the first place, the Community is producing ever-increasing surpluses. To finance them holds down more and more finance needed elsewhere. It is therefore being criticized as uneconomic and must discredit our Community in public opinion, especially as the consumers feel that they are being pushed on one side.

Beyond this, if this development continues it will exceed our financial capacity. We are also encumbering the world agricultural markets with our surpluses, and this we must avoid out of regard for world trade. For this reason we must, not only for economic and financial reasons but also for political, make strenuous efforts to overcome the problem of surpluses. In any case this needs a basic reform of the instruments of agricultural policy, of the market regulations.

Secondly, the functioning of the agricultural policy is also impeded because each of our countries is faced by unsolved structural problems in the agricultural field. The solution of these is urgently necessary if we wish to arrive at balanced structures of our overall economies. They, on the other hand, are a prerequisite for the necessary economic harmonization at Community level.

The reform of the agricultural structures will, however, have to remain to a large extent our Governments' own responsibility. Experience shows that even the individual Governments' structural policy tasks have to be delegated to "lower levels". What is crucial is, that we all determinedly continue the structural policy and coordinate it in the way that is demanded by the growing together of our national economies.

So that here and at the discussions in the coming weeks there are no misunderstandings, I must also say quite frankly that I have to represent not only the interests of the German taxpayers but also the future of the German farmers. My programme of internal reforms includes an agriculture that is modern and competitive.

This is the framework in which, in our view, the problem is placed. It follows that the Federal Government is able to agree to a financial settlement in the final phase only if it is certain that the consultations on the surplus problem, e.g., on the reform of the agricultural market regulations, are immediately initiated and are energetically pursued on the basis of ideas promising of success. All Member Governments must require their representatives in the Council to push on energetically with the work in company with the Commission. Nor, in this connection, will there be any taboo on the existing function of the prices. We need a prompt settlement making it possible for us to appreciate in good time the obligations we should assume.

Only so would the Federal Government be able to recommend to the legislative bodies that they should agree to the financial arrangements. The need for these arrangements results from Ordinance 25/62, which expressly envisages the introduction of the process pursuant to Article 201 of the EEC Treaty.

Naturally the German Bundestag also sees an internal connection between agricultural financing and enlargement. Under this aspect I have noted with satisfaction pronouncements of other Governments that, particularly in view of the enlargement of the Community, the agricultural system, including the financial arrangements, must remain capable of adjustment.

If we can come to an agreement on these lines, the way would be open for a settlement of the final agricultural financial arrangements. The Commission has submitted to the Council proposals which, as a whole, have for this a special importance. However, none of us will be unable to realize that in the coming weeks and months we shall nevertheless be confronted by very hard individual decisions.

IX. With regard to these deliberations, I would like to add, about the attitude of my Government, that we have to make a choice between a bold step forward and a dangerous crisis.

I am saying here nothing different from what I am saying at home: that the people of Europe are waiting and pressing for the statesmen to place the will to succeed at the side of the logic of history. Europe needs our success.

If I again draw attention to the younger generation it is to tell you of the Federal Government's wish to set up a European Youth Organization. We are feeling encouraged by the—on the whole—very good experiences we have made with the Franco-German Youth Organization.

In the sphere of world politics, our consolidating and expanding Community ought to pursue a dual role: by combining our resources, Europe should be enabled to make headway against the super-Powers, economically, scientifically and technologically, and in this way to preserve its identity. At the same time it should enable Europe energetically to co-operate in the great task urgently facing the industrial countries—development aid policy.

We can render no better service to our ideals—peace and humanity.

Communiqué of the Conference of the Heads of State and Government of the EEC Member States on December 1—2, 1969, at The Hague

1.   On the initiative of the Government of the French Republic and at the invitation of the Dutch Government, the Heads of State and Government and the Foreign Ministers of the EEC Member Countries assembled on December 1 and 2, 1969, at The Hague. On the second day, the Commission of the European Communities was invited to participate in the business of the conference.

2.   In view of the impending entry into the final phase of the Common Market, they expressed the opinion that it is the duty of the holders of the supreme political responsibility

in the Member States to draw up a balance of what has been achieved hitherto, to proclaim their determination to continue this work, and to draft the guidelines for the future.

3. In retrospect, they stated that doubtless never before have independent States realized a more extensive co-operation and were unanimously of the opinion that, precisely because of the progress that has been made, the Community has now reached a turning-point in its history. Considerable political importance therefore attaches to the end of the year as a date, apart from the resultant technical or juristic problems. Entry into the final phase of the Common Market means not only the acknowledgment of the irrefutability of what has already been achieved by the Communities but also the pioneering of the way to a united Europe able to assume its responsibility in the world of tomorrow and to make the contribution that is appropriate to its tradition and its mission.

4. The Heads of State and Government therefore confirm their belief in the political aims that bestow on the Community its entire purpose and its significance. They proclaim their determination to carry on with their work to the end, and they stress their confidence in the ultimate success of their efforts. If a remarkable source of development, of progress and culture is not to be exhausted, if the equilibrium in the world is to remain preserved and peace guaranteed, it is their common opinion that a Europe embracing States whose essential interests coincide with the preservation of their national character is inevitable, a Europe that is conscious of its own cohesion, that stands by its friendship with other States and is aware of the tasks devolving upon it: to promote international détente and understanding among nations—first and foremost, among the nations of the entire European continent.

The European Communities remain indisputably the nucleus from which European unity has developed and received its impetus. The accession of other countries of our continent to these Communities, pursuant to the modalities envisaged in the Treaties of Rome, would doubtless help the Communities to reach dimensions corresponding more and more to the present level of economy and technology. The creation of special links with other European States which have expressed such a wish should also help towards this end. Such a development would allow Europe to remain true to its open-to-the-world tradition and to redouble its efforts on behalf of the developing countries.

5. In view of the completion of the Communities, the Heads of State and Government have confirmed the will of their Governments to proceed from the transitional period to the final phase of the European Communities and, consequently, to lay down the final fiscal arrangements governing the common agricultural policy at the end of 1969.

They have agreed, within the framework of these fiscal arrangements, and taking all possible interests into account, to replace step by step the contributions of the Member States, under the procedure outlined in Article 201 of the EEC Treaty, by their own revenues, with the aim of arriving, at the agreed time, at a complete financing of the budgets of the Communities; they also agreed to increase the budgetary powers of the European Parliament.

The question of direct election will be given further study by the Council of Ministers.

6. They invited the Governments energetically to continue in the Council the efforts already undertaken for a better control of the market by an agricultural production policy that allows for a restriction of the burden on the budget.

7. The acceptance of a fiscal ruling for the final phase does not exclude its adaptation, to be taken in hand unanimously, particularly to an enlarged Community, in which case, how-

ever, the principles of this ruling must not be debased.

8. They confirmed their will to forge ahead more rapidly with the further development necessary for the strengthening of the Community and its development to the economic union. They consider that the process of integration must result in a Community of stability and growth. For this purpose they are agreed that a phased plan for the establishment of an economic and monetary union is worked out in the Council in the course of 1970, based on the Council's Memorandum of February 17, 1969, and in close collaboration with the Commission. The development of the co-operation in monetary matters should rest on the harmonization of the economic policy.

They are agreed to let the possibility of the institution of a European Investment Fund be examined which would have to lead to a common economic and monetary policy.

9. They confirmed their will to intensify the technological activity of the Community and to coordinate and promote, especially through Community programmes, industrial research and development in the important top-ranking spheres and to earmark therefor the necessary finance.

10. They also consider fresh efforts are necessary in order to work out at an early date a research programme for the European Atomic Energy Community, framed according to the requirements of modern industrial management, that shall make the most effective employment of the Joint Research Centre possible.

11. They again proclaim their interest in the creation of the European University.

12. The Heads of State and Government consider timely a reform of the Social Fund within the framework of an extensive harmonization of social policy.

13. They confirm their agreement respecting the principle of enlarging the Community, as envisaged in Article 237 of the Treaty of Rome.

As far as the States prepared to accede accept the Treaties and their political aims, the consequential legislation that has materialized since the commencement of the Treaty and the options taken regarding the development, the Heads of State and Government have approved the opening of negotiations between the Community and the States prepared to accede.

They were agreed that preparations indispensable for the working out of a common basis of negotiation can be carried out within the most helpful and the shortest time; according to unanimous opinion these preparations shall be made in a very positive spirit.

14. As soon as the negotiations with the States prepared to accede have commenced, talks will be initiated with the other EFTA Member States expressing a wish for this on their relationship with the EEC.

15. They commissioned the Foreign Ministers with the examination of the question how, in the perspective of the enlargement, progress could best be achieved in the area of political unification. The Ministers will make proposals on this before the end of July, 1970.

16. The measures here agreed for the creative framing and growth of Europe open out the prospect of a larger future if young people closely associate themselves with them; the Governments have borne this wish in mind and the Communities will give this matter their attention.

Statement of the Federal Government on the EEC Summit Conference at The Hague, made by the Federal Chancellor on December 3, 1969 before the German Bundestag

Mr. President, Ladies and Gentlemen,

At the opening session of the summit conference at The Hague the day before yesterday, I—clearly alluding to public opinion here at home and in this Honourable House—said that we Europeans had to choose between a bold step forward and a dangerous crisis. This choice has been made.

I can state with satisfaction that the European Community Heads of State and Government assembled at The Hague have decided in favour of the European future. We succeeded, with all difficulties about which we must clear, in overcoming the paralyzing stagnation of the European development and making the way clear for the development and enlargement of the Community. With this, Europe has a fresh opportunity. I even say: with this, Europe has a great fresh opportunity.

Here before this Honourable House my thanks are owed not least to the Dutch Prime Minister, de Jong, who, as President, conducted this conference with circumspection and energy. They are owed in the first place to the French President, Georges Pompidou. Without him and his courageous attitude we should have failed. The course and the outcome of the conference were abundant proof of Franco-German friendship. The French President and the German Federal Chancellor were at one in thinking that our Europe must be prepared to accept the challenge of the '70s. But, of course, without the solidarity of Italy, the Netherlands, Belgium and Luxembourg we should similarly have been denied success.

President Pompidou had taken the initiative for this conference this summer. He found the right moment—namely, a few weeks before the date on which the European Economic Community enters the final phase of its development as conceived in the Treaties of Rome. We all know how important interim results have been achieved in the meantime; nor, in this connection, would I like to omit mentioning here the name of a Member of this Honourable House, Professor Walter Hallstein.

But we also know how very much in recent years the European development has been retarded and, not least, through the unresolved question of the accession of other States, particularly the United Kingdom, which were, and are, prepared to accept the principles laid down in the Rome Treaties as well as the consequential European legislation and to acquire full membership.

The Federal Government was never able to endorse—and changes of Government have altered nothing, or almost nothing, of this attitude—former, very decided reservations on the part of the French Government towards an enlargement of the Community. This period and this dispute are over. France has approved the early assumption of negotiations between the Community and the States prepared to accede and hopes—as we—for a successful outcome of the negotiations. Anyone who listened to the French President at the conference has to say with conviction: we have confidence in the given word.

These negotiations on entry will commence in the middle of next year at the latest, and they will have to be conducted by the Community in the spirit that envisages a successful conclusion and can then also guarantee it.

We have also stated that, directly after the commencement of the negotiations with the States prepared to accede, talks will be carried on with the other EFTA countries about the establishment of a special relationship with the EEC.

Ladies and Gentlemen, at least as important is this: The Heads of State and Government have commissioned the Foreign Ministers with a re-examination of the question of political unification in Europe and, moreover, in the perspective of the enlargement. A report on this is to be submitted by the middle of next year.

I regard this the *core* of the outcome of the summit conference because it makes two things clear: the qualified political co-operation is one day to result in Western Europe being able to make its appearance in world political connections with one voice, and it is to be enriched quite soon by the prospective participation of other countries in this process of coming nearer to one another politically.

The European, and particularly the German, people have rightly awaited with growing interest—here and there, also with anxiety—the decision taken at The Hague in the question of the accessions. And rightly, I can certainly say, has the Federal Government, have the Foreign Minister and I, made the solution of this question a focal point of our efforts because it was a key issue for the treatment of other subjects as well. Without success in this sphere, the European stagnation could not have been overcome; in other words, the conference would have been doomed to failure.

It was, in our opinion, in the very nature of things that a connection should exist between the question of entry and the questions of the completion and deepening of the Community and this had to be made clear. But here it was not a question of concessions that, as with a closure of business, the advocators of one standpoint had to make to those of others. We too, the we who have so strongly championed the enlargement in the interest of Europe, are interested no less than France and others in the completion and deepening of the Community. Here too I can state with satisfaction that together at The Hague we succeeded in making progress which will determine not only the immediate, but also the distant, future.

Ladies and Gentlemen, as far as the coming weeks are concerned we have jointly undertaken to settle the final financial ruling of the common agricultural policy by the end of this year, in which connection it is not to be excluded that the clock can be, and perhaps must be, stopped a little. We shall fulfil the obligation under the Treaty—and that is what matters: the commitment under the Treaty—, but we shall naturally bear in mind not only the general interests of the Community but also those of a sound production policy, of an overcoming of the problems of surpluses, of a rational management of public money and, above all, the interests of our farmers.

Moreover, I made clear at the conference that a modern German agriculture able to compete forms part of our own programme and that the structural policy in the agricultural sphere must remain in the hands of the Federal Government. Unlike the financing of agriculture, the reform of the agricultural policy stands on the Community's agenda. The need to ratify the fiscal arrangements by our legislative bodies is uncontested. It has also been recognized that, in connection with the enlargement of the Community, the agricultural policy must remain to a certain degree capable of adaptation.

As far as the other perspectives of European co-operation are concerned, the will to develop the European Community further to form an economic union was obvious at The Hague. That cannot be achieved without a convergent economic policy. The aim is the carving-out of an economic union. Growing from small things to large, the principle of solidarity must one day be fully effective. It is a matter of course that solidarity in monetary and economic policy can be achieved only if we actually arrive at a common policy of growth and stability open to the world. We have decided that the Council, in close co-operation with the Commission, shall work out a phased plan in the course of 1970 for the establishment of the economic and monetary union. And then, in this connection, the possibility of setting up a European Investment Fund is also to be examined . . .

In this connection I have also gained the impression—I hope I can say this without exaggeration: one must naturally avoid exaggeration, and I always go to great lengths to do so—that, after many setbacks and disappointments, a European consciousness directed towards the future is growing, and is not exhausted, as so often, in the settlement of procedural questions. To this extent we can now appear before the younger generation in our country and say that of course it would have been possible to imagine more, but that what could have taken place now has taken place and that decisions have been taken on matters on which a decision was possible. The difficulties still facing us must not be overlooked, but the European idea has received new impulses, and that is good.

Moreover, the proposal to create a European Youth Organization on the lines of my Government statement has also a chance of being implemented.

The Community's institutions form the political scaffolding for the European building. It was important that yesterday the President of the Commission participated in our deliberations. The Commission and the Council in Brussels will have important services to render both with regard to the enlargement of the Community and to the internal structure. They must therefore be given the possibilities to operate more effectively. The fiscal arrangements will promote the Community's independent management of the budget, and it necessarily follows—and this has been promised— that the powers of the European Parliament will be strengthened. Now, this extension of the Parliamentary competencies and of Parliamentary control is fortunately no longer in dispute.

Ladies and Gentlemen, today I would like with this initial statement about the decisions of the conference at The Hague to leave it at that. The Federal Government presumes that the Foreign Committee in particular attaches importance to a detailed report. Naturally the Federal Government places itself immediately at disposal whenever the House should so wish.

Allow me to summarize: It has been possible to avert a crisis in the Community. It has been confirmed that Europe is not merely a technical term, but that it is a political task to which the Governments are addressing themselves. It has been seen that at a moment when a struggle is going on for a new relationship between the World Powers, between the great nuclear giants, and when much is astir in the world, the Europeans are capable of putting forth fresh efforts.

I have, of course, always proceeded from the premise that fresh efforts in Europe—and for ourselves, whenever it is possible, better relations between Eastern and Western Europe— must be firmly embedded in a consolidation of the coherence of the Western European States.

With regard to the position of our Federal Republic, the Federal Government is not, therefore, unclear about its position within the circle of our allies and partners; nor are our allies and partners unclear. We shall move heaven and earth to make sure that the new beginning recognizable at The Hague does not result in no further progress . . .

Speech of the Federal Minister for Foreign Affairs, Walter Scheel, before the German Bundestag on February 25, 1970 (Excerpt)

Since the beginning of December, we, together with our partners in the EEC, have adopted a large number of basic Resolutions for what is called the completion of the Community, and thus for the still-outstanding arrangements of the customs and agricultural union and for the financing of the overall integration. The period of transition is thereby ended, and the

Community, about the existence of which serious anxieties had to be entertained only a few months ago, has now entered the final phase. With this, we in Western Europe have now definitely left the confrontation of the States and their interests behind us, and their full interdependence has been reached. This development must sooner or later lead to a complete economic and monetary union. The Honourable House knows that the Federal Government has proposed, and worked out, a phased plan for achieving this aim. Even this present year such a plan is to be approved by the Community and constitute the core of what, as the French call it, the "deepening of the Community".

For France, the Resolutions on the completion of the Community were a prerequisite for the initiation of negotiations on accession with the United Kingdom, Denmark, Norway and Ireland. Replying on the given word, we on our side have refrained from making any conditions in this matter.

Nothing now stands in the way of the initiation of the negotiations on accession. For this reason we wish to conclude as quickly as possible the discussions in Brussels on the establishment of a common negotiating position of the Community so as to be able to start negotiations with all applicants for entry before the summer recess. Then, at the proper time we shall have to make an approach to the other European States whose economic interests are also, in the end, inseparably associated with ours.

At the summit conference, the Federal Government submitted our proposal on political co-operation in Europe, which was included as Point No. 15 in the final communiqué. With this, the stagnation—in the sphere of political co-operation as well—has been overcome and the decision made to arrive at last at the co-operation in developing foreign policy considered by all of us as urgently necessary. The preparatory talks are under way, and at the next session of the EEC's Council of Ministers this question will for the first time be dealt with in greater detail on the fringe of the formal session.

Speech made by Federal Chancellor Willy Brandt at a Luncheon of the Foreign Press Association at the Dorchester Hotel, London, on March 3, 1970 (Excerpt)

One important subject is, of course, the question of the accession of the United Kingdom to the European Community. You know that the Federal Government has always advocated this accession, as also that of other States. This is also in accordance with the prevailing attitude of our people, as shown by all public opinion polls. I myself consider the outcome of the summit conference at The Hague the most important foreign political event during the period in which I have been Head of Government. There, it proved possible to overcome the European stagnation. We must now make sure that the momentum is maintained, that the development continues positive.

In the coming months, the Six, in company with the Commission, will prepare for the commencement of the negotiations on entry. These negotiations will have a bearing on many intricate technical questions and not be free from complications.

However, as long as we all stick to the conviction that the Community must be enlarged so that Europe can assert itself politically, economically and technologically, these difficulties can be overcome. The enlarged Community accords with the common interest in a consolidation and a solidarization in our part of the world.

This is, if I leave the conference at The Hague out of account, my third official visit abroad since I became Head of Government. A month ago I was in France. A good Franco-German relationship is important for Europe. In 1946, Winston Churchill said that the first step towards the re-foundation of the European family must be a partnership between France and Germany. That still applies. After my trip to France we had the visit of the Irish Foreign Minister, and then I was in Copenhagen. The Swedish Foreign Minister will be coming to Bonn in the next few weeks. I myself shall be in the United States at the beginning of next month and then be visiting Norway and Italy as well.

This enumeration by itself shows how interwoven the European countries are and how close the association across the Atlantic is. My talks up to now, and those of the Minister for Foreign Affairs, have been encouraging. We proceed on the assumption that progress is being made with the integration of Western Europe. We believe that the prerequisites are present to allow the Atlantic Alliance to remain effective. We are also glad that the Eastern components of our European policy have met with understanding.

As you know, we are endeavouring to fill in the rifts between the countries—towards the East as well. I regard this as an important service we can render Europe. All that lies in our power will be done, so that Germany cannot be called, from whatever side, a mischief-maker. Germany's foreign policy has become more logical, more unbiassed—if you like—in her policy of peace and policy of détente. I believe that this has been widely understood.

It lies in the interest of the whole of Europe that our Governments should normalize relations with the peoples of Eastern Europe. I beg you not to forget that the Federal Republic has a certain leeway to make up in this connection. Our aim is that Bonn should maintain normal relations with, for example, Warsaw and Budapest, such as other Western countries also have.

We have started a dialogue with the Soviet Government and have assumed a thread of conversation with Warsaw. We are also endeavouring, in the relationship between the two German States, to arrive at a modus vivendi in the interest of the people and in the interest of peace. The Federal Government hopes that its contact with the Government in East Berlin will bring us a step forward.

Speech of the Federal Chancellor at the National Press Club in Washington on April 10, 1970 (Excerpt)

Nor are we Europeans always free from uneasiness when it is a matter of our dependence. The idea of European unity has been actively put into practice within the framework of the European Economic Community. The enlargement of the European Community will now make progress, after many years of stagnation. The aim of the European idea is not only to end once and for all the epoch of internal conflicts in Europe, but also to set Western Europe on its own feet, since only in this way can we become full partners and cease to be for ever partial boarders.

European integration is, and remains, the central element of a policy pointing ahead and serving the preservation of peace. My Government is promoting it with all the means at its command. And today I can give a clear answer to the question whether this integration is making progress. Yes, that is the case; we are making progress.

In this connection I am not sure whether here in America it has been properly understood everywhere what the European summit conference at The Hague at the beginning of last December signified and what—as I may hope—will be the result. By this I mean:

- We have decided to develop and enlarge the European Community.

- The way has therefore been opened for negotiations with the United Kingdom and other States prepared to accede.

- In this connection the Franco-German friendship has withstood an important test.

- The preparations for political co-operation in Western Europe, which have been stagnating since 1962, have now been resumed.

- Our American friends who in the post-war years pleaded so vigorously for the unification of Europe need no longer be disappointed but, with us, can gather hope from the fresh developments.

But—it can be held against me—, will not an enlarged EEC come into conflict to a greater extent with the trading interests of the United States? This would be so only if we in Europe isolated ourselves. But that would be contrary to our own interests. The Federal Republic of Germany will vigorously urge that the European Community must not be an impediment to worldwide liberalization. The growth of our own economy demands this.

There have been less convincing tendencies. However, it can already be stated that experiences so far have not been so trying.

Allow me to recall that trade between the United States and the Community trebled from 1958 to 1969, that in 1969 the United States' trading surplus with us amounted to 1.2 billion dollars, that today the EEC has the lowest and the most balanced customs tariff among all trading partners, and that the Community is still the most important market for America's farm produce.

There are other questions, particularly those that result from existing or prospective associations or special agreements with the EEC. We are able to point to political necessities. In the United States the fear still lurks that the consequence will be discriminations. In order to be able to speak about such and other questions objectively and continuously, I recommend closer contacts between the EEC and the United States.

Address by Federal Chancellor Willy Brandt before the Parties Represented in the Norwegian Parliament on April 24, 1970 (Excerpt)

In Germany there has been no making light of the experiences of the past. In the Federal Republic we have laid the foundations of a democratic and social State based on the rule of law. In the meantime a new generation is beginning to assume the responsibility for nation and State. We have not forgotten that the road to European and international co-operation was paved so rapidly for us, nor that—here in Norway as elsewhere—there were many who so early discarded the feelings of hostility and mistrust and treated us with understanding and a readiness to help.

We must not forget the lessons of the past. But it is necessary to direct our gaze ahead. History has set the peoples of Europe a new challenge, which could be the last: to establish a peace order for our continent which makes it possible for the peoples in this part of the world to have an assured future and which can at the same time be a model and a means to help peoples in other parts of the world. We must all make a contribution towards this.

This peace order—as see it, and as my Government sees it—embraces both the relations of the Western peoples among each other and the connection which we, in the light of the common responsibility resting on all the peoples of this continent, are seeking to make with the peoples of Eastern Europe. Both these tasks belong together like the two sides of a coin.

For me, there is no separation of the policy towards the West from the policy towards the East. For me, what is called German *Ostpolitik* is capable of development only against the background of the Atlantic Alliance and in conjunction with the integration of Western Europe. Formulated in general terms: the close association of the States of Western Europe among each other is the precondition for finding the strength to establish such effective—and, if possible, trustful—relations also, as ought to be matter of course, irrespective of the different political systems, in recollection of the common cultural roots and in the awareness of the continuing common responsibility for the members of this continent.

Only a successful policy towards the West makes it possible to pursue this policy towards the East; conversely, a continual pursuit of the policy towards the West is part of a successful policy towards the East. This formula exposes the internal connection which, for my Government, exists between the two halves of this policy.

From this connection it follows, for me, that it is right if—if possible—all peoples of Western Europe have a hand in both components of this policy. If they were separated, their powers are rendered ineffective. If all of them—with the differences of ways necessarily taken into account—are associated with the West European integration, this already means an important step in the direction of the future all-European peace order. In this connection I wish to make it unmistakably clear that I do not regard the Western European alliance as being either an isolationist market or as a rigid structure benumbed by ideas of blocs.

In terms of world politics, only a pacified and united Europe will be able, in the future development, to assert itself politically, economically, socially and technologically alongside the super-Powers and thereby preserve its own character and productive power. Only such a Europe will be able so to employ its creative capacities that the living conditions of the poorer peoples of this earth can be improved effectively. A united Europe that no longer squanders its finest energies on internecine strife could find herein the mission for its 21st century.

Today, it is easier for me to develop before you this vision of the future, now that in recent months the Western European policy has been activated and even the East-West relations are displaying not merely negative factors.

The summit conference of the six EEC countries at The Hague last December put an end—as far as the West is concerned—to years of stagnation. The political will to make progress towards what is contractually described as "increasingly closer integration of the European peoples", which has been lacking for so long, found expression in numerous constructive decisions.

This applies quite particularly to the decision of the Six this summer to initiate negotiations with the States which are prepared to accede. I assume this will be possible by the end of June or the beginning of July. Nor will this be in respect of the United Kingdom only.

Now, however, please believe me when I say that I have not come here to try to recruit members. Norway will herself know at the proper time how to decide what best serves her interests.

I will only say that the Federal Republic of Germany would welcome the enlargement of the EEC. And I will repeat that I do not regard this as being a solely British problem. For me, there is no doubt that the European Community would be well served by, particularly, those fresh impulses which it can derive from Scandinavia. Added to the economic productive power and social vitality, the Commission could well do with the democratic and moral calories from the North.

I cannot understand the fears that a smaller nation might lose its identity in the Community, that it could be overwhelmed by the superior power of the larger Member States. The fact is that, thanks to its system binding on all, the Community safeguards rights and possibilities, particularly those of its smaller Member States, in such a manner as is not otherwise found in international co-operation.

Already the Community includes Member States of varying size, populations and economic power. Each of them can delegate one or two members to the Commission with the same right as the larger. So far as majority decisions are envisaged—and in an enlarged Community these must play a larger part than up to now—, the principle applies that the votes carry weight only in conjunction with the principle of State equality. Therefore, within the framework of the Community, a smaller State can exercise an influence which has far greater consequence than accords with its economic power and population.

In these stipulations is expressed the appreciation that the period of struggles for the leading role in Europe must be a thing of the past. The Treaties of Rome seek to imply that, for us, the Europe of hegemony no longer exists. For us, it is a matter of a Europe of equality and of mutual regard in which it is no longer the will of the strongest that prevails but the strongest argument no matter by which side it is put forward.

Allow me to repeat that I have not undertaken to deliver a recruiting speech. But allow me to add that we should not ignore what the younger generation is expecting of us. If I understand the young people aright, they want not only added prosperity but, above all, the creation of more humane forms of coexistence. They will say yes to Europe all the more easily if this—I confess in the light of the long march of the reforms—is synonymous with the fresh start to a higher degree of justice and greater stability.

If negotiations on entry should start this summer it will be clear, on the one hand, what common negotiating position the present EEC partners have worked out and, on the other, that the States prepared to enter will develop their ideas in an initial round of discussions. The Six have not yet worked out a negotiating position vis-à-vis Norway, but it can be assumed that the Community is very familiar with the special problems that are exercising Norwegians' minds in connection with the accession issue. And I hope it will not be too difficult to find solutions that are satisfactory to all concerned . . .

I need not tell you how important it is that we in Europe make quicker progress in the sphere of technological co-operation. And I am glad that Norway is prepared for active participation.

I would like, however, to stress that in the sphere of actual foreign policy and security we must make greater efforts to harness all the energies of Western Europe and so exercise a stabilizing influence on world political events. This is in no way inconsistent with our commitments within the Atlantic Alliance, and it is certainly in no way directed towards a divorcement from the United States. On the contrary, it is directed towards more personal responsibility, towards partnership and equality.

As President Nixon made clear in his message to Congress on February 18, and as he confirmed to me in our recent talks, the development of the European Community continues to meet with the full support of the United States. To the extent that Europe is invigorated by a harnessing of its forces will it also be able to assume greater political responsibility in the interest of all.

In this connection, there must be no blinking of the fact that an expanding Common Market—which is being developed into an economic and monetary union—is not entirely without problems for America as well. Even though the EEC is not directed inwardly, but will give a considerable stimulation to world trade, American trading interests will not remain unaffected in one sphere or another. In order to avoid unnecessary conflicts and to decide unavoidable points of controversy objectively, I have recommended regular contacts between America and the Community.

Interview of the Federal Chancellor with the "PPP" (Parlamentarisch – Politischer Pressedienst) on May 9, 1970, marking the 20th Anniversary of the Publication of the Schuman Plan

Question:

Twenty years ago today, on May 9, 1950, the declaration of the French Government which has made history under the name "Schuman Plan" was made public. What significance do you attribute, in retrospect, to this declaration?

Answer:

It is one of the truly creative achievements of our times. Because of it, Robert Schuman, just as his then advisor Jean Monnet, deserves enduring thanks. I see its singularity in two elements:

1. Especially for democratic States the framing of relations towards former wartime enemies is particularly difficult because account has to be taken of the emotions of public opinion. The magnanimity with which France, in the Schuman Plan, offered the defeated Germany a fresh and close association contrasts with earlier historical experiences. The declaration therefore produced the shock effect that was required to deliver our two nations from their centuries of sanguinary entanglement.

2. With his Plan, Schuman departed from the models of classic co-operation between independent States by proposing placing, in a limited but vital area, coal and steel production, the resources of both peoples under a "joint supreme supervisory authority". Thus had been realized for the first time the so productive idea of the independent community organ furnished with its own rights. With the choice of coal and steel, Schuman wished at the same time to make any new war materially impossible. Understandably, this aspect particularly appealed to the ideas of people weary of war.

France's preparedness to sponsor such a policy of equality of status ushered in a fundamental change in the relations between two nations. On this soil it was possible for the prospering of the reconciliation which, initiated by Robert Schuman and placed by General de Gaulle on a broader basis, led to the self-evident friendship now linking us with France under her President, M. Pompidou.

Question:

Do you see in the Schuman Plan the inception of the "United States of Europe", and would you be prepared to accept the resultant consequences?

Answer:

In point of fact the Plan represents in a nutshell the starting-point of the march to

Europe. However, Schuman too was clear that this march could be neither short nor rapid. In his declaration of May 9 it says, characteristically: "Europe cannot be established at one blow, nor by a simple concentration".

For us too this still applies, even if we have since made considerable progress in the construction of Western Europe. However, what I tried a short while ago to formulate as follows is almost a truism: The coming generation will have to do the rest. The dovetailing of the centuries-old European nations can take place only step by step through a gradual extension of the areas in which a common policy is possible. What in this connection is crucial is that the process is continuous and spirited, since standing-still is equivalent to retreating.

Question:

With this the approach, wherein do you see the ultimate aim?

Answer:

I belong to a political party whose programme ever since 1925 has been tied up with the United States of Europe. And no one will imagine me to be a thorough-going nationalist who rejects, say, supranational authorities or a State organized on federal lines. But we have simply not yet advanced so far that it is possible already to fix the ultimate aim in all details. Why should we allow ourselves already to be forced into the traditional international categories of such alliances when here—as everywhere in the European construction—there exists so much room for the creative reframing! Moreover, we all know from experience that every over-hasty crystallization can be damaging.

What is certain is that the European Community sees its aim in political union. In the EEC Treaty this is expressed with the cautious but dynamic formulation of an "ever closer alliance of the European peoples". The task we

are set, and to which the Federal Government addresses itself with energy, is quite simply to press ever forward on the road towards this close alliance, until at last the point is reached where the final form becomes visible and can be fixed.

Question:

How in this connection do you judge the events of recent months?

Answer:

For the Federal Government, the summit conference at The Hague was a turning-point. We had assumed office shortly before. Our expectations and fears were clearly outlined in the Government policy statement of October, '69. The Federal Minister for Foreign Affairs and I allowed a great deal of care to be taken with the preparation for the conference, and the results achieved with our initiative have confirmed that the concentration on attainable, concrete results was right.

The decisions taken at The Hague go far beyond the arrangements which, with the approval of the Bills by the Federal Government last Wednesday, have now been submitted to the legislative bodies for ratification: the Community's fiscal arrangements and the strengthening of the European Parliament's budgetary powers. In the coming weeks and months the Federal Government will undertake further steps in which the political will for progress demonstrated at The Hague comes to expression.

I would like to invite all the people in our country interested in Europe—whether they are entrusted with it within the scope of their political party work, bear the responsibility for it in public administration, or have committed themselves to it voluntarily—to assist in achieving that the impetus we were able at The Hague to inject once more into the European movement continues to have effect in the new efforts. For us Europeans, 1980 is to be the year by which union will have to be reached in the areas of economic and monetary policy, structural assimilation, social harmonization and rounding-off institutionally.

Question:

What chances for political co-operation do you see?

Answer:

Quite good chances—because even in this point we were able at the summit conference at The Hague to make a new start. After all the disappointing experiences with previous efforts towards a European Political Community and a Political Union, it will now be a matter of developing an effective consultation mechanism. This should, on the one hand, lead to the formulation of common views via the coordination and the gradual approximation of standpoints and, on the other, it should be capable of developing gradually, on the lines of a consolidating co-operation, into the Union or the Community. In this way we are creating something more concrete than if we were neglecting what is nearest to hand through placing our wishes on too high a level. The Federal Government will certainly not lag behind others, but with every step we must endeavour to reach agreement with our partners.

Question:

The CDU/CSU has been alluding recently to the danger that the Federal Government may be neglecting integration in Western Europe on account of its policy towards the East. How does this tally with what you have said?

Answer:

It does not tally because this assertion is totally inapt. Actually I am wondering how such a false way of looking at things can arise with us, as in other countries this view is never put forward. The concrete behaviour of the Federal Government at Brussels clearly speaks for the opposite. Our policy towards the East demands an activation of the policy towards the West because the latter has to be embodied in the former. Our German policy towards the East is looked upon as forming part of Western Europe's coordinated policy towards the East and it is, for its part, to be seen in the bonds of alliance with the United States. From this co-operation flows, in my opinion, a further strong argument that we must advance more quickly in Western Europe.

The integration of Western Europe should be regarded in an all-European perspective. The European Community considers itself not as an association for West Europeans who are satisfied with themselves but as a system in this part of Europe which needs an organic link with the East European States. After all, all European peoples bear a common responsibility for peace and the development of our continent. In this sense the Federal Government's policy towards the East and its policy towards the West are elements in a German foreign policy forming one whole; it strives for a pacified and united Europe in which Germany too can find her place.

The final goal of the European construction cannot be reflected better than by a quotation from the Schuman Plan of twenty years ago. It said: "A contribution that an organized and active Europe can render to civilization is indispensable for the maintenance of peaceful conditions."

Reply of the Federal Government to a Major Question of the Parliamentary CDU/CSU Party on the Policy towards Germany, the East and Europe of May 6, 1970 (Excerpts)

The aim of our policy is that the Federal Republic of Germany, as a member of the European Communities and partner in the Atlantic Alliance, renders her own contribution to the creation of a peace order in Europe. The purpose of this peace order is also to combine the hitherto separated European States into a new, greater whole. This is a process that calls for the patience and good will of all concerned. Only within this framework does the Federal Government see realistic possibilities for bringing the two German States into contact with one another.

The continuity and further development of earlier approaches characterize the Federal Government's policy directed towards this goal.

Towards the West, we are able to link up with the years of successful steps along the road leading to the integration of Europe. The Federal Government has made the determined continuation of these approaches its matter, particularly in the prospect of Europe's political unification. Its contribution to the summit conference at The Hague, to the conclusion of the transitional period of the European Community, and to its deepening and enlargement, proves the success of a policy which convincingly combines essential aims with justified interests.

Towards the East, already former Federal Governments had indicated their interest in a policy of reconciliation. All parties in the German Bundestag are united in the wish to overcome, by negotiations, a position of confrontation which has to be at the expense of the people in Eastern and Western Europe. If through its initiative the present Federal Government has opened out greater possibilities

along the road than its predecessors, this does not mean that at the bottom of it lies a change in the aims of German policy. What has, however, changed is the intensity of the efforts to reach a settlement in Europe. The outcome of these efforts will show whether or not the preparedness of our conversation partners in the East to seek a peace order through negotiations has grown.

The Federal Government can continue its policy of peace only if it is certain of the co-operation and support of her conversation partners and allies. To this extent, German policy towards the West and German policy towards the East are inseparably associated. Just as, towards the outside, co-operation in the West is a precondition of our freedom of action, so do we, towards the inside, need a broad measure of approval for initiatives. The Federal Government will therefore remain concerned to secure the approval of all who, together with it, follow the aim of rendering a peaceful contribution towards overcoming the confrontation in Europe ...

Already the Federal Government has explained several times in detail before this Honourable House its policy towards Europe, lastly on April 16. In doing so it has time and again emphasized its commitment to press ahead as energetically as possible with the completion of the task of European integration. What has been achieved in the brief span of policy towards Europe since the autumn of 1969, particularly since the summit conference at The Hague on December 1—2, 1969, and not least on German initiative, is documented by the following data:

Political Co-operation

December, 1969—January, 1970:

Soundings by the Federal Government of the five European Community partners about the way in which to initiate the operations in implementation of Point No. 15 in the final communiqué at The Hague.

End of January, 1970:

Circulation of an aide-mémoire containing our idea about the political co-operation and putting this forward for discussion.

February, 1970:

Continuation of the bilateral soundings about the political co-operation.

March 6, 1970:

Meeting of the six Foreign Ministers for a first discussion of the political co-operation. The Political Directors are commissioned to prepare the second meeting of the Ministers, which takes place on March 28—29, 1970, at the invitation of the Italian Government.

April 14, 1970:

Discussion of the six Political Directors at The Hague.

May 11, 1970:

Discussion of the Political Directors of the six Foreign Ministries in Brussels.

EURATOM, Technological Co-operation

December 6, 1969:

Meeting of the Council of the European Atomic Energy Community; Resolution on the activity of the Joint Nuclear Research Centre: it is to be made an independent establishment, with modern management and the incorporation of non-nuclear activities.

October 28, 1969:

Council Resolution; invitation to other European States, particularly in view of the enlargement of the European Community, to participate in technological co-operation on the basis of the Aigrin Report.

EEC Sphere

The Council occupied itself with the "packet" agreed at The Hague for completing the Community at its sessions on, among other dates,

December 8—9, 1969
December 15—16 (extended to 22), 1969
January 19—20, 1970
February 5—6, 1970
March 6—7, 1970
March 20, 1970.

At the Council sessions on April 20—22, 1970 (General Council) and April 27—28, 1970 (Agricultural Council) this packet was approved by the following Resolutions:

April 20—22, 1970

1. Fiscal Arrangements

● Ordinances on agricultural financing (transitional and final arrangements)

- Resolution on the replacement of the Member States' contributions by own revenues (ratification needed)
- Resolution on preview of finances over several years
- Resolution on the control of the agricultural markets
- Resolution on the regulation of certain transitional problems arising out of the reorganization of the previously existing fiscal system.

2. Agreement on amendments to the Community Treaties with reference to the budgetary powers of the European Parliament (ratification needed).

3. Arrangements in the Tobacco Sector

- Ordinance on the creation of a marketing organization for raw tobacco
- Resolution concerning the consumer tax on tobacco goods except the turnover taxes
- Resolution concerning the State monopoly on trade in tobacco goods.

April 27—28, 1970:

Formal approval of the world marketing arrangements, on which basic agreement had already been reached in the session on April 20—22:

- Ordinance concerning the marketing organization for table wine
- Ordinance concerning the marketing organization for quality wine
- Basic Resolutions concerning the most important questions for the issuing of regulations with particular reference to the framing of prices.

To give more depth to the Community, the Federal Government, at the Council meeting on January 26, 1970, submitted a "phased plan" for realizing the economic and monetary union in the EEC. At the meeting of the Council on March 6—7, 1970, the plan, together with plans submitted by Belgium, Luxembourg and the Commision, were handed over for dealing with by a committee consisting of the presidents of the Member States' competent committees for economic, fiscal and monetary policy and a representative of the Commission headed by the Luxembourg Prime Minister and Minister of Finance Werner which will submit a report at the end of May, 1970.

For the enlargement of the Community, the Council on December 8—9, 1969, drew up a list of subjects for working out a common basis of negotiation of the six Member States. Already at the Council meeting on April 20—22, 1970, agreement had been reached on some of the subjects.

The following are the answers to the individual questions:

Question 1:

Is the Federal Government committed to the final aim of a Federal State? Is it prepared to propose a phased plan containing a binding "action and time" programme for the early realization of a political union embracing foreign and defence policies?

Answer:

This Federal Government has repeatedly and unambiguously emphasized that our efforts towards European integration are aimed not at a union of economic interests but at political unity. At the summit conference at The Hague the Federal Government therefore urged that considerable progress be made in political unity via the completion of the Common Market, its enlargement by new members and increasing its depth. This German initiative found expression in Point No. 15 of the final communiqué at The Hague.

We have learned from the past that perfectionist plans for a Political Union can be a hindrance to concrete progress. Under these circumstances it must for us be a matter first of all of overcoming the stagnation in the sphere of European political co-operation that has in practice existed ever since 1962. We succeeded in doing that at the summit conference at The Hague. At the present time, all six of us are searching for possibilities for setting political co-operation in motion in the perspective of the enlargement of the European Community. Without wishing to minimize the services of our partners in this direction, it can be said that the ideas worked out by the Federal Government and circulated as an aide-mémoire at the beginning of this year represent an essential basis for the comprehensive exchange of opinions taking place at the present time.

All partners are assuming that, with the political co-operation that is sought, it is first of all only a matter of a first phase of the development towards a Political Union. In the light of experience and the development of conjointly responsible political attitudes we shall have step by step to pass new Resolutions on the intensification of the co-operation in the direction of the aspired goal. To this extent it is possible to speak of a phased plan, even if neither the individual stages nor the dates when they will be realized are defined.

Question 2:

Does the Federal Government share the view of the Parliamentary CDU/CSU Party that the group of members of the European Economic Community and Political Union must be identical?

Answer:

The Federal Government takes the view that, basically, only members of the European Economic Community can participate in European political co-operation on the lines of Point No. 15 of the Protocol of The Hague. It would, however, welcome it if the States prepared to accede could already during the nego-

tiations be included in the political co-operation in a manner acceptable to all.

Question 3:

Is the Federal Government prepared to say unequivocally that accession to the European Community presumes the approval of the final political aim and that therefore links other than accession must be found for neutral countries?

Answer:

Like the Opposition, the Federal Government takes the view that accession to the European Community presumes the approval of its ultimate political aim. The efforts for European integration are directed towards the political aim, as is expressed in the Preamble of the EEC Treaty. Therefore, the acceptance of this aim is one of the essential preconditions of membership. This is recognized by the countries who have made application for entry.

European countries which have not made such application will themselves decide whether or not they can approve this aim and the preparedness to surrender sovereign rights necessarily associated therewith. If they cannot or do not wish to do so, the Federal Government will be concerned within the framework of the Six to safeguard another and appropriate form of participation of these countries in economic co-operation in Europe.

Question 4:

Does the Federal Government share the view that the active development of the European Communities demands the extension of the integration to further areas and the strengthening of the institutional structure of the existing Communities?

Answer:

Apart from a few individual areas which are at present under discussion in the Brussels

Community bodies, and in respect of which arrangements are impending, the Community has fulfilled the obligations imposed upon it by the EEC Treaty and the legislation deriving from it. To this extent we can, therefore, speak of a "completion" of the Common Market. However, the development during the past years has shown that with this the Community cannot stand still. The deepening of the Community must be urged forward on a broad front. The central task for the future is, thereby, the creation of an economic and monetary union. For this, solutions going beyond the requirements of the customs union will have to be found. Only so can what has so far been achieved be safeguarded in the future as well.

Already on January 26, 1970, the Federal Government submitted to the Council a phased plan for the realization of the economic and monetary union. The Federal Government is participating with great intensity in the deliberations on this plan which have since been initiated.

The Federal Government continues to be of the opinion that in a growing Community the organs must remain to a particular extent capable of arriving at a moulding of unanimous will. Naturally the need for a flawless functioning of the institutions results especially from the development of the Community into the economic and monetary union as well as from the aspired enlargement of the Community. In this connection it is first of all a matter of the organs acting in unison in conformity with the Treaty. Moreover, in the view of the Federal Government the Treaty (or the Treaties on the founding of the individual Communities) certainly contains possibilities for a strengthening of the institutions which are not yet fully exhausted. On the basis of the Treaties, the Federal Government, together with its present and future partners, will remain concerned to preserve and to consolidate the institutional preconditions for a harmonious development of the Community.

Question 5:

What is the position with regard to the "working out of a common basis of negotiation" envisaged for the accession of new members in the communiqué of The Hague?

Answer:

Already with the working out of a common basis of negotiation for the negotiations on accession the Council of the European Communities has made good progress. The Member States are agreed that States acceding must approve the Treaties and their political aim, the consequential legislation that has originated since the Treaty started to operate, and the options taken respecting the development.

On the basis of this agreement, a list of subjects, agreed on December 6, 1969, is under thorough discussion in the Council of Ministers of the European Communities. Agreement has already been reached on the following topics:

- Transitional arrangements;
- Questions in connection with the enlargement of the Community in the light of the economic and monetary union;
- ECSC problems.

At the two forthcoming Council meetings, the following subjects will be up for discussion:

- Commonwealth questions;
- EURATOM;
- Institutional questions;
- Negotiating procedures.

Apart from this there is agreement that a common negotiating position towards those EFTA States which wish for economic co-operation with the enlarged Community must also be worked out.

We have justified grounds for believing that the necessary common basis for the negotiations on accession can be approved at the second meeting of the Council in June.

Question 6:

Is the Federal Government prepared to advocate in particular a strengthening of the European Parliament and an extension of its powers?

Answer:

The Federal Government continues to advocate a strengthening of the European Parliament. This it has proved in recent months. The Federal Government takes the view that a strengthening of the powers of the European Parliament is all the more necessary the more the powers of the national Parliaments are assumed by the Communities. These naturally also include legislative powers. The Federal Government also takes the view (shared by all Member States) that, in the case of the arrangements, now for ratification by the Member States, on an extension of the European Parliament's budgetary powers appropriate to the stage of development in which the Community finds itself at present, it is a matter of a provisional ruling. It is obvious that no institutional equilibrium is reached as long as the budgetary and legislative powers of the European Parliament are out of balance.

In order to consolidate the democratic basis of the Community and to embody it still further in the consciousness of the population of the Member States, the Federal Government continues to support general and direct elections to the European Parliament. It has therefore been playing an active role in the consultations within the Community in recent months.

Question 7:

Does the Federal Government share the view of the CDU/CSU that the fears entertained in many places that the Federal Government's policy towards the East can lead away from the concrete policy of European integration must be countered not by words alone but by concrete proposals?

Answer:

The Federal Government does not recognize any antagonism between the policy towards the East and the policy towards the West. If its initiatives in the matter of the policy towards the East have had an effect on the policy towards the West, then this has consisted in a strengthening of the efforts for European integration. The connections of the practical steps taken in connection within the framework of these efforts have already been described in detail.

The connection between the policy towards the East and the policy towards the West is, moreover, not a subject of negotiation for the Federal Government; nor will it in future be given up nor restricted.

Statement of the Federal Minister for Foreign Affairs on July 20, 1970, at the Opening of the Session of the European Communities' Council of Ministers in Brussels on the Occasion of his Assumption of the Council's Presidency (Excerpt)

Since The Hague, much has happened. But particularly in the next six months we shall be faced with a large number of new tasks. The internal development and the external enlargement will necessitate our taking a very large number of decisions in the coming months. In close contact with the permanent representatives and the Commission, the Council will have to address itself with energy to its operations...

There is no alternative to this programme. Europe must play its part in the worldwide concert of States. Thereby the Community must not isolate itself, either in its relations with its European partners or with other continents. The position reached in the international division of labour must be maintained. Further progress in worldwide co-operation is necessary. For this, Europe is called upon to build bridges and reduce the tensions in the world. This also needs our common efforts in the next six months.

Address of the Parliamentary State-Secretary with the Federal Chancellor, Dr. Katharina Focke, before the "Europa-Union" in Stuttgart on July 29, 1970 (Excerpt)

IV. If we now turn to the present state of integration in Western Europe, the starting-point must be that the European Community is, and remains, the crucial instrument. Even though at first it was possible to realize it only as an economic community, it nevertheless represents the first and most extensive realization on the road to political unity in Europe. This aim has been repeated in all clarity in the communiqué of The Hague. Thereby the six States have reconfirmed, for themselves and for the future members, the political goal of the European community.

In the course of the thereby fixed development process, the political co-operation, as now to be taken in hand in implementation of Point No. 15 in the communiqué of The Hague, naturally represents only an initial approach to the goal of political unity. All the same, the Member States will undertake to engage in a regular consultation on questions to do with foreign and security policy, and not only to harmonize their views but also to strive for common action. At the same time they will also decide that this co-operation must be developed step by step in the direction of full political unity.

This advance, the first since eight years of stagnation in the foreign policy sphere, must be seen within the overall context of the political resuscitation of the Community idea. An enlarged and deepened Community and political union belong together, and even if first of all in agreement among the members in an organizational and structural manner, their organizational connection is nevertheless to be seen, since this step is a logical development. Until it is possible to realize the final goal of a Europe on a federalistic basis, sought equally by the Federal Government, the parties forming it and the Opposition party, many interim stages will still be required. What is crucial is that the first step it is possible to take has been taken.

V. At The Hague, the Heads of State and Government set the EEC itself the threefold task of completing the transitional period of the Common Market, the deepening and the enlargement of the Community. The steps connected with the completion have already been taken. The replacement of the Member States' financial contributions by their own revenues and the strengthening of the budgetary powers of the European Parliament represent the most positive result. The most serious crisis the Common Market has yet experienced broke out in 1965; now, this central element has at last been regularized on community lines. The Community's budget will now be entirely separate and independent of the national contributions. This means that the Community acquires the same financial independence as is possessed by any State.

Certainly the new controlling powers granted the European Parliament are by no means so sufficient that it is possible to speak of a genuine budgetary law, but at last, after many fruitless quarrels, a start has been made which can, and must, be developed. The review of these powers within two years, already laid down, demonstrates the direction of the development.

In the control of the agricultural markets, the hoped-for progress has not yet been made, but we all know that the incorporation of the farming community in a socially satisfactory manner in an industrial society with its division of labour is socially and politically extraordinarily difficult. It is possible to find the solution only in a determined attack on the structural problem. This is a tremendous task. Whether or not it can be mastered on the principle that structural matters remain a national competence seems uncertain in the long run.

The recuperation of the European agricultural structure comes already within the sphere of the deepening or the internal development of the Community. The need for the internal development results from numerous considerations of which here I want to mention only one: the interdependence of the national economies has reached a degree which allows disturbances in one Member State to affect the economy of other Member States much more directly than formerly; on the other hand, the divergence in the economic policy of the individual Governments is still so wide that, as we have recently twice experienced, they are forced to take corrective monetary policy measures in order to restore the balance.

Only the establishment of the economic union, already envisaged in the Treaty, offers a way out of this vicious circle; all further consequences which are occasionally hinted at, such as the re-nationalization of the agricultural markets, would conflict with the Community Treaties and mean a setback when everywhere progress is needed.

Here the summit conference at The Hague took crucial decisions on binding steps to point the way: the basic policy decision to realize the economic and monetary union with the help of a phased plan. With the proposal of the Federal Minister of Economics of February 12, 1970, the Federal Government has given the discussion a notable incentive. The "Werner Committee", the responsible body for these matters, has already submitted an interim report; the final report will follow in September. It is not in dispute that within a period of ten years the Member States wish to break through to a full union closely resembling a European Federal State.

There can be no doubt that progress towards an economic and monetary union as a result of the influences exerted on all others by this central area will mean decisive progress. However, at the same time we must also be aware that in its turn this progress depends on measures taken in other areas.

A common taxation policy is a prerequisite for the implementation of a common economic policy. A progressive economic and monetary union also demands a balanced industrial structure. This naturally also includes common research and technology in order to diminish, or even to start to fill, the gap between Europe and those who are leading in this field in the world.

It seems to me that the preparation of a common regional policy has been far too neglected, particularly in this connection. The dynamics acquired through private initiative in the Common Market have not sufficed, as the liberal school tends to assume, to balance out the regional structural differences among the individual parts of the Member States and the Member States as a whole. Up to now the lack of balance between regions concentrating on industry and regions concentrating on agriculture has by no means been redressed. I believe the time has come to attack regional policy in a much more determined fashion than has hitherto been the case.

The common social policy also needs a correspondingly energetic attack. At Saarbrücken Federal Chancellor Brandt put forward the demand that the Community should become the world's most progressive area socially, even in this present decade. This involves, among other things, the existing European Social Fund also becoming an instrument of a balanced employment policy. Here too the Federal Government has come forward with active commitment and its own initiatives; on the lines of a well-understood solidarity, it wishes under the German presidency to achieve a successful outcome of this reform for the Community's socially underdeveloped regions—in the Federal Republic as well.

I do not want on this occasion to talk about the need to arrive at a common policy in other spheres as well in, for example, particularly trade, power and transport. I merely wish to stress that the common guidelines I have just mentioned will call for the institutional strengthening of the Community's organs. The shifting of crucial technical competencies on to them is compelling all the organs to organize themselves more rationally, more representatively and more effectively. This includes, sooner rather than later—according to us—general, direct election to the European Parliament.

VI. The internal development and the enlargement are interrelated. Only if the internal development, together with the negotiations on entry, is continued with all tenacity of purpose, will no one need to fear any longer that the enlargement will weaken the Community. Conversely, we know that the internal development cannot be effected without an enlargement.

On the other hand, the opening of the negotiations on entry in the first days of December at The Hague, on precisely the date contemplated by us, demonstrates how much confidence obviously exists among the Community countries. Decisive for this has been not least the loyal and generous attitude of the French Government in recent months. For the first time, the prospect has opened out that the Europe of the Six can be transformed into a Europe of the Ten. At any rate the Community

of the Six has made all the necessary arrangements in good time and comprehensively.

It has proved possible to work out rapidly a satisfactory basis of negotiation for the Six. The Federal Government can claim to have been conducive towards, on the one hand, preserving the degree of integration already achieved and, on the other, leaving the applicants for entry sufficient room to negotiate. As a starting-point, in accordance with the communiqué of The Hague, the four applicants have stated their preparedness to approve the Community Treaties, their political aim, the consequential legislation created since the Treaty started to operate, and the options relating to the development that have been agreed.

Here I do not wish to examine the Community's individual decisions but only allude to some of the most important. These include that, in the view of the Community, the necessary adaptation must be made with the aid of short-term and balanced transitional measures; a change in the existing regulations has meanwhile been agreed. In the case of the agricultural questions—crucial for the applicants for entry—, the Six are agreed that the bases of the common agricultural policy must not be jeopardized. Nor must the principles governing the social arrangements be adulterated when adapted to the enlarged Community.

There can be no doubt that herein lies one of the greatest difficulties for the negotiations, especially since the present British Government's White Paper has included the wish that the United Kingdom should pay a fixed share amounting to a maximum of 15 to 20 per cent. of the total Community costs instead of the transfer of levies, customs duties and part of the value added tax receipts. However much the Community must have an understanding of the aspect of limiting Britain's financial burden—since we ourselves can have no interest in exceeding the limits which Britain is able to pay—, there can be no question of concurring in an exception which clearly contradicts the principles on which the Community is founded. But I am convinced that the desire for success is everywhere present and that it will enable this obstacle to be surmounted.

For the EFTA countries not wishing, or unable, to accede, the Community has, on principle, contemplated solutions which, except for those not confirming to the GATT, must primarily meet the requirement that no new trading obstacles are set up in Europe.

It cannot be excluded that in the course of the negotiations the Community will be exposed even more than up to now to the criticism that it is acting contrary to the aims of a liberal world trade and, in particular, that it is impinging on the basis of the GATT, the most favoured nation principle. In recent times this criticism has been repeated, and even exaggerated, particularly in the United States. However, in the case of the various preference agreements of the Community it is not be to countered completely, even through fully respecting the GATT rules, since even if the large preference area thereby arising is directed towards a customs union or a free trade zone it is not exactly pleasing to America's economic interests.

The responsibility of the Community, as the largest partner in world trade, entails that it must take this aspect into account as far as possible. At the same time, the political responsibility to be assumed by the Community demands that it gives every assistance to the economic—and therefore also the political—stability not only to the States and regions with traditional economic and political relations with one of the Member States but also to those countries which are in need of special relations because of their economic orientation towards the Community—the Mediterranean countries, for instance—who wish for this and are, moreover, thrown back upon it in order to maintain their independence. It will be necessary to try to secure American understanding of this by alluding to the distribution of world political burdens which have to eventuate between the United Europe and America as the West's strongest member.

With a view to this balance, the Federal Government has advocated a continuous dialogue as comprehensive as possible between the Community and the United States.

VII. All in all, a good half year after The Hague the European Community can be seen in a gratifying light, in a light that recalls the "Golden Years of European Promoterism" at the beginning of the '60s. The commitments entered into at The Hague have been met on time. New commitments must follow. Nowhere more than in European integration does standing-still mean setback—and only constant progress guarantees the necessary speed of development. I believe that all forces in the Federal Republic well-disposed towards Europe should, together, and without qualification, help to see that this speed is maintained.

Address of the Federal Minister of Food, Agriculture and Forestry, Josef Ertl, on October 2, 1970, in the Japanese Ministry of Agriculture in Tokyo (Excerpt)

II. Two important factors characterize the situation we see facing us today in the European Economic Community.

Agriculture is the sphere in which the integration of the six Member States is the most advanced. Pursuant to Article 39 of the EEC Treaty, the aim of the common agricultural policy is to increase agricultural production, to guarantee the agricultural population an appropriate standard of living, to stabilize the markets, and to ensure provision and delivery to consumers at appropriate prices.

Of the possible forms of organization envisaged in the Treaty for the establishment of a uniform home market for farm produce—common rules concerning competition, coordination of the individual countries' marketing organizations, a common European marketing organization—the form of the common European marketing organization is the one that is almost exclusively in operation. In the meantime, about 95 per cent. of all farm products are covered by marketing organizations which, despite varying forms, have three things in common: uniform prices, the practising of a common trading policy towards Third Countries, and the granting of sales preference within the Community for home-grown products on the basis of financial solidarity.

This extensive and politically important integration process in the agricultural sphere has not so far been matched by similar progress in the spheres of economic, market development and monetary policy. In the EEC, prices are fixed uniformly for the Member Countries. However, since these still have their own individual currencies, it was necessary to create what are called "units of account" for the agricultural prices of all Member Countries. This unit is based on the American dollar and is often, therefore, called the "green dollar".

The incompatibility between, on the one hand, the mechanism for adjusting these units of account and, on the other, the inevitable fluctuations in the exchange rates due to the Member Countries' market development policies was clearly shown with the devaluation of the French franc and the upward revaluation of the DM in 1969. At the time it demanded great efforts on the part of the Federal Government to secure agreement in the competent EEC bodies about an offsetting of the revenue lost by German agriculture and to safeguard the

price stabilizing effect of the lowering of producers' prices in agriculture connected with the revaluation.

For these reasons, in the next few years the most urgent aim in internal Community policy will be to achieve a similar degree of integration in the other sectors mentioned to that already existing in the agricultural sphere. However, in this respect there will be many problems to solve. It must be taken into account that agriculture is part of the economy as a whole and that it is impossible to subject only one part to strict common rules—and particularly common prices—without also assimilating the price-forming factors mainly determined in the other sectors of the economy. It is, therefore, a particular concern of the German Government in the Council of Ministers to see that progress is now made in the common economic, market development and monetary policies as well.

In observing the present situation, the second factor that catches the eye is the fact that in the EEC over-production prevails in the case of the most important agricultural products, with the EEC's agricultural market regulations frequently being made partly responsible. You are certainly not unaware that in recent years in the EEC quantities—in some cases substantial—of grain, butter, skimmed milk powder and sugar have had to be stored because production exceeded sales. This development resulted in a growing financial burden on the Member Countries, although in no improvement in the incomes of the persons engaged in agriculture, and created ever-greater difficulties in the policy of trade with Third Countries.

I shall go into this latter aspect in greater detail later on. Before then, however, I would like to take a brief look at the situation that will result from the planned enlargement of the European Economic Community.

The EEC is at present engaged in negotiations with the United Kingdom, Ireland, Denmark and Norway on an accession of these countries to the Community. The success or failure of these negotiations will help to a great extent to determine Europe's economic and political future.

From the aspect of agricultural policy it would certainly have been more proper to have taken this step already in 1963. Then, there were no structural surpluses, no problems so acute and momentous. Now, this Community of the Six has to enter into negotiations on accession with these problems unresolved—a circumstance that will certainly not facilitate the negotiations although, on the other hand, we shall not have to be frightened of them. I believe that both the EEC and the countries that are prepared to accede know exactly what this is all about.

The world political events after the failure of the first negotiations on accession in 1963 are likely to have shown all concerned that the European States had to act, that for Europe there is no other alternative promising of success.

We, together with the countries prepared to accede, shall be dealing with the unresolved problems of the old Community. This means, for instance, that the efforts to secure a uniform economic and monetary policy will have to be extended to the countries now joining and pursued with the greatest seriousness, since the probability of a monetary correction among Ten is greater than among Six. Furthermore, an EEC of Ten will have to take difficult hurdles in its internal agricultural marketing policy and its trading policy towards Third Countries.

One very crucial problem will be whether or not the enlargement of the Community will lead to a reduction in the agricultural surpluses. If the only country to enter is the United Kingdom, and thus a market which has to import about half of the food consumed, a decrease in the present surpluses and a relief for the future could certainly be expected. However, in this connection it is possible that, at the same time

as the United Kingdom, Denmark and Ireland, and thus two countries with agricultural surpluses—particularly in animal products—will also be entering, and this will necessarily have an effect on the supply situation in the enlarged Community. Much will also depend on whether or not there will be an increase in production in the countries acceding after assuming the EEC's price levels; this is a danger that cannot be excluded, at least in the case of certain products.

You see that in this respect many questions are still open, and it is, therefore, very difficult to draw conclusions. However, with regard to the problem of surpluses it is already possible to say that in the case of certain types of goods reliefs are to be expected; in the meantime, the overcoming of all the difficulties is scarcely likely to be achieved through the enlargement of the Community . . .

III. I hope that with these observations I have made it clear that it is by no means the aim of the Community in the sphere of trading policy to assert its position in the world with a policy of protectionism or autarky. The Community— and here the Federal Republic of Germany particularly—is one of the largest importers of foodstuffs and at the same time one of the most important exporters of industrial products. Moreover, it is aware that it can maintain this position only if it pursues an open-to-the-world policy, that is, if it renders its contribution to the advancement of world trade both for industrial and for agricultural products, a contribution that must, of course, be based on reciprocity.

The open-to-the-world attitude of the Community is a fundamental concern of German policy. Moreover, it has also found expression in the Treaty establishing the EEC, where, in Article 110, it says: "Through the creation of a customs union, the Member Countries intend, in the common interest, to contribute towards the harmonization of the development of world trade, the removal step by step of the restrictions in international trading transactions, and the lowering of customs barriers."

Through the creation of a standardized agricultural market, the EEC Member Countries have realized a first phase of its development. This first phase must now be complemented and further developed, the long-term aim of the European Economic Committee being to become a genuine political union.

As an important partner in world trade, it will try to achieve an ever-closer economic co-operation with the other partners in world trade so as, in this manner, to achieve greater progress than hitherto in creating prosperity and thus in the final analysis in preserving peace.

Report of the Foreign Ministers to the Heads of State and Government of the Member Countries of the European Communities, submitted on October 27, 1970, in Pursuance of Point No. 15 of the Communiqué of the Conference at The Hague of December 1—2, 1969

Under the chairmanship of the Federal Minister for Foreign Affairs, Walter Scheel, the Foreign Ministers of the six European Community States finally passed, on October 27, 1970, in Luxembourg, in the name of their Governments, the report submitted on July 22, 1970, in pursuance of Point No. 15 of the communiqué of The Hague.

The following is the text of the report:

First Part

1. The Foreign Ministers of the Member Countries of the European Communities were commissioned by the Heads of State and Government, meeting on December 1 and 2, 1969, at The Hague, to examine the question "how, in the perspective of the enlargement" of the European Communities, "progress could best be achieved in the area of political unification".

2. In fulfilment of this task, the Ministers were at pains to preserve the spirit of the communiqué of The Hague. The Heads of State and Government confirmed, in particular, that, with the entry into the final phase of the Common Market, Europe had reached "a turning-point in its history"; they stated that "the European Communities remain indisputably the nucleus from which European unity has developed and received its impetus", and they finally expressed their determination "to pioneer the way to a united Europe able to assume its responsibility in the world of tomorrow and to make the contribution that is appropriate to its tradition and its mission".

3. The Heads of State and Government stressed: "If a remarkable source of development, of progress and culture is not to be exhausted, if the equilibrium in the world is to remain preserved and peace guaranteed, it is their common opinion that a Europe embracing States whose essential interests coincide with the preservation of their national character is inevitable, a Europe that is conscious of its own cohesion, thas stands by its friendship with other States and is aware of the tasks devolving upon it: to promote international détente and understanding among nations—first and fore-most, among the nations of the entire European continent."

4. Conscious of its responsibility arising out of its economic development, its industrial potential and its standard of living, the united Europe is willing to redouble its efforts for the

benefit of the developing countries in order to establish trustful relations among the nations.

5.   The united Europe must rest on the common heritage of respect for freedom and human rights and be an association of States with freely elected Parliaments. This united Europe remains the virtual aim that must be achieved as early as possible through the political will of the nations and the decisions of their Governments.

6.   Therefore, in order to preserve the continuity and political objective of the European plan, the Ministers take the view that their proposals must start from three considerations.

7.   First consideration: In the spirit of the Preambles of the Treaties of Paris and Rome, the will to political union that has increasingly promoted the progress of the European Communities must take shape.

8.   Second consideration: The practical implementation of the common policy clearly pursued, or in preparation, in certain areas calls for corresponding developments in the actual political sphere in order to bring the time when Europe can speak with one voice nearer; for this reason it is important to proceed with the building of Europe in successive stages, and step by step to develop the most sensible method making possible a common political action.

9.   Final consideration: Europe must make preparations to exercise the responsibilities to assume which it is not only committed but also compelled because of its added cohesion and its increasingly important role in the world.

10.   The present development of the European Communities demands that the Member States should intensify their political co-operation; in an initial stage they must create the practical conditions so that they are able to harmonize their ideas in the sphere of international policy.

It seems, therefore, to the Ministers that first and foremost common efforts are required in the sphere of coordinating the foreign policy in order to demonstrate before all the world that Europe has a political mission. The Ministers are convinced that a suitable step in this direction would be to promote the further development of the Communities and so give the Europeans a livelier awareness of their common responsibility.

Second Part

The Ministers propose the following:

In the endeavour to achieve progress in the sphere of political unity, the Governments are determined to co-operate in foreign policy.

I.   Aims

This co-operation has the following aims:

- to guarantee a better reciprocal understanding of the great issues of international politics through the regular supply of information and through consultations;
- to encourage the harmonization of standpoints, the coordination of attitudes and, where this seems possible and desirable, common action, and thereby strengthen solidarity.

II.   Ministerial Meetings

1.   On the initiative of the currently officiating President, the Foreign Ministers convene at least once every six months. Instead of the Ministerial meetings, a conference of the Heads of State and Government can be convened if, in the view of the Ministers, this is justified by grave circumstances or the importance of the subjects up for discussion. In the event of a serious crisis or particular urgency, an extraordinary consultation will be held between the Governments of the Member States. The currently officiating President contacts his colleagues to decide on the best methods to guarantee this consultation.

2. The Federal Minister of the country taking the chair in the Council of the European Communities presides at the meetings.

3. The Ministerial meetings are prepared by a committee consisting of the Directors of the Political Departments.

III. The Political Committee

1. A committee composed of the Directors of the Political Departments convenes at least four times a year in order to prepare the meetings of the Ministers and to carry out the tasks set it by the Ministers.

The currently officiating President can, after consulting his colleagues, also convene the Committee on his own initiative or at the request of a member for an extraordinary session.

2. The chairmanship in this Committee is arranged in accordance with the chairmanship in the case of the Ministerial meetings.

3. The Committee can set up working groups for special tasks.

It can commission a group of experts to gather material about a specific problem and outline possible solutions.

4. If necessary, any other form of consultation can be considered.

IV. Consultation Subjects

The Governments consult each other on all important issues of foreign policy.

The Member States can propose any issue they please for political consultation.

V. The Commission of the European Communities

To the extent that the operations of the Ministers affect the activity of the European Communities, the Commission is invited to express an opinion.

VI. The European Parliamentary Assembly

In order to give the political unity a democratic character, the public and their represen-tatives must share in it. The Ministers and the members of the Political Commission of the European Parliamentary Assembly meet twice a year for a colloquy on questions which are objects of consultation within the scope of the foreign political co-operation. This colloquy will be informal in order to make it possible for parliamentarians and Ministers to express their opinions freely.

VII. General Provisions

1. As a rule the meetings are held in the country whose representative presides.

2. The host country provides the secretariat and the material for the prosecution of the meeting.

3. Each country nominates an official of its Foreign Ministry as conversation partner for his colleagues from the other countries.

Third Part

1. In order to guarantee the continuity of the action that has begun, the Ministers will examine how further progress can best be achieved in the political unity; they intend to submit a second report.

2. This examination also includes the improvement in the foreign political co-operation and the search for other areas in which progress might be achieved. It will have to take into consideration the operations undertaken within the framework of the European Communities, above all such as are directed towards consolidating their structures and, in case of necessity, to put them in such a condition as to measure up to the extension and development of their tasks.

3. For this purpose the Ministers commission the Political Committee to frame its work so

that it can fulfil this task and to make a report to them at each of their half-yearly meetings.

4. The currently officiating President of the Council addresses a communication on the progress of this work once a year to the Parliamentary Assembly.

5. Notwithstanding the possibility to submit interim reports, the Foreign Ministers, if they consider this necessary and the state of the investigations so permits, submit their second general report two years at the latest after the commencement of the foreign political consultations. This report is to contain an evaluation of the results achieved through the consultations.

Fourth Part

Proposals on the co-operation of the States prepared to accede in the operations dealt with in Parts II and III of the report.

1. The Ministers stress the connection between membership in the European Communities and participation in activities to facilitate progress in the sphere of political unity.

2. Since the States prepared to accede will be consulted about the aims and procedures described in this report and will have to make them their own, it is necessary, as soon as they become members of the European Communities, to keep them informed on the development of the operations of the Six.

3. In view of these aims, the following procedures are proposed in order to ensure the informing of the States prepared to accede:

(a) Meetings of the Ministers

At each of their half-yearly meetings, the Ministers fix the date of their next meeting.

At the same time they fix the date to be proposed for a meeting of the Ministers of the Six. As a rule, this should, as far as possible, be near the date of the meeting of the Six; in this connection, consideration is to be given to the occasions when the ten Ministers, or some of them, otherwise meet.

After the meeting of the Ministers of the Six, the officiating President communicates to the States prepared to accede the points which the Ministers propose for the agenda of the Ministerial meeting of the Ten and gives all further information which is suited to make the exchange of views as productive as possible.

In view of the fact that a certain flexibility must characterize this informing and the exchange of views, it is assumed that it will be extended after the treaties of accession have been signed by the States making application to join the European Communities.

(b) Meetings of the Political Committee

The Political Committee supplies the States prepared to accede with the information that might interest them. The information is communicated by the currently officiating President, who also accepts possible reactions of these States. The President reports in this connection to the Political Committee.

Statement of the Federal Chancellor before the German Bundestag on November 6, 1970, on the Federal Government's Policy towards Europe (Excerpt)

For this decade the Federal Government has set five objectives in particular:

- the early enlargement of the Community by the States prepared to accede,
- the establishment of the economic and monetary union which is to extend and complement the Treaties of Rome,
- to develop the now commencing political co-operation in Western Europe in such a way that a political community can result,
- to establish the partnership of the Community with America and to assume appropriate responsibility in world politics, and not least
- to follow up the possibilities, existing at any particular time, of communication and co-operation with the countries of Eastern Europe and to put them to good use in the general interest.

One of the most important advances of the last twelve months is the initiation of negotiations with the countries prepared to accede. The Federal Government is proceeding on the assumption that the negotiations, which are making good progress, will lead in the shortest possible time to a satisfactory outcome—that is, to the full membership of the United Kingdom and the other countries.

The accession of these countries will increase the economic strength of the Community, promote its social development, and strengthen it politically. The negotiations with the countries seeking some other form of association with the Community are now starting up.

Here, too, the Federal Government will do what it can to ensure that these negotiations are pursued energetically.

The great common task of the '70s is to develop the Community further into an economic and monetary union. Here, in company with our partners, we must take determined steps into the future. In reality, the phased plan worked out by the Six together with the Commission represents a new Magna Carta for the Community. This means, among other things, that the integration of Europe must not be misunderstood as an integration in favour of the highest prices ruling at any one time.

Extensive institutional reforms are required. The economic and monetary union will have to be linked with the long-needed strengthening of the Community's institutions. The Parliamentary controlling organ must be strengthened. It ought also, in the development lying before us, to be able to result from general, direct elections.

At all events, the Federal Government is ready to follow this road and, together with its partners, to set a time limit for the carrying out of the necessary tasks. The economic and monetary union will ensure growth and stability in the larger area. If it is to develop its usefulness to the full, this union will have to be accompanied by progress in other areas. This includes, to mention only a few important complexes, the reform and development of a comprehensive European policy on technology going beyond the Treaties of Rome, the overcoming of the—in part still marked—differences in individual regions of the Community, an assimilation of the educational policy, and a progressive European social policy, the aim being to make the Community, in this decade, the truly most progressive large area in the world.

Measures which are suited to make the essence and the advantages of the Community visible and tangible for the individual citizens in the Partner States seem to me to be urgently necessary. One measure in this direction would be the abolition of the frontier controls in the tourist and goods traffic.

Here too the Federal Government will be at pains once again to set others a good example.

It is also urgently necessary for us to harmonize projects for internal reform in the Community countries and to develop common ideas. In this connection, it is not only a matter of bringing living conditions into line. Europe must, in any case, be more than the drill-ground of a technocracy whose exercises can only with difficulty be understood by the people in our countries.

Yesterday the Federal Cabinet discussed the position attained with the build-up of the Community and laid down our line of march. I can say without any exaggeration that we shall remain on the initiative, as we always have been.

Now at last the political co-operation is also set on foot. It is good that on October 27 in Luxembourg the six Foreign Ministers passed their report submitted pursuant to Point No. 15 of the communiqué of The Hague.

With the forthcoming meeting on November 19 in Munich, a mechanism for foreign political consultation between the Member States of the Community will be set in motion for the first time since 1962 . . .

Statement of the Federal Minister for Foreign Affairs, Walter Scheel, at a Press Conference on the Occasion of the Consultations of the Foreign Ministers of the Six Member Countries of the European Communities on November 19, 1970, in Munich

I am convinced that this Foreign Ministers' meeting represents a decisive stage on the road to Europe's political unity. As German Foreign Minister, I am particularly happy that it was possible to hold this first consultation on German soil. It underlines the priority the Federal Government assigns to the policy of European integration.

With this conference, a process of an ever-closer foreign political co-operation among the six Community countries is set on foot. At it, the four candidates for accession also participated in a manner acceptable to them. It is effectively connected with the European Parliament and the Commission of the European Community. With it, at last the step which Europe has endeavoured unsuccessfully to take in the past has been taken.

At their conference at The Hague on December 1 and 2, 1969, the Heads of State and Government commissioned the Foreign Minis-ters with the examination of the question "how, in the perspective of the enlargement", the European Communities "can best achieve progress in the area of political unification". The Ministers have punctually fulfilled the commission set them. They have worked out a phased plan for Europe's political unity. Within this plan, first of all the initial stage was defined. We are realists. To brood on the impossible, to clothe it in fine-sounding phrases, brings us no further. On the other hand, to tackle the possible, to transform it into reality, means progress.

For the initial phase of political unity, a consultation mechanism is visualized. The Political Committee, composed of the Political Directors of the six Foreign Ministries, meets at least four times a year. It prepares the Ministers' consultations and deals with the tasks assigned it by the Ministers. The Foreign Ministers meet at least once every six months. When grave circumstances or the importance of the subjects up for discussion justify it, a conference of the Heads of State and Government can be convened instead. Extraordinary consultations at the level of the Ministers and the Political Committee are also envisaged. The chair is taken by the Foreign Minister or the Political Director of the country presiding in the Council of the European Communities.

The consultation mechanism initially does without a rigid, pre-settled institutionalization. This was also out of consideration of the candidates for accession. However, the procedure itself includes the necessary *rudiments* of a pragmatically progressive institutionalization. These clearly make their appearance in the report, in the Political Committee, and in the nomination of an official of the Foreign Ministry concerned as the responsible conversation partner. In this manner the Ministries will be "short circuited".

As for the consultations themselves, the Ministers have agreed to keep them confidential. I know that this does not facilitate your tasks as journalists. It is, however, indispensable. We do not want any shouting from the housetops. We mean business.

With our eyes on these aims we have agreed to provide the diplomatic representations in Third Countries and with international organizations with an identical instruction laying down the procedure for close co-operation at diplomatic level as well. We have also taken care that the multilateral co-operation between our Foreign Ministries envisaged in the report is initiated. In future, the procedure will be that a country which wishes to inform its partners on topical and important events no longer does this in the traditional bilateral manner but requests the representatives of the Ambassadors of the five EEC countries to come and be informed *together* on the spot. Should another Foreign Ministry wish to react to such information, by, say, commenting on it or complementing it, this in its turn is effected in the multilateral manner I have outlined. In addition, in each Foreign Ministry and in each Embassy of the Member States of the European Community a certain official will be entrusted with the execution of tasks arising out of the report. Thereby a close and efficient network guaranteeing the continuity and effectiveness of the foreign political co-operation beyond the consultation mechanism has been created.

We know that today we have taken a first step in the right direction. One day Europe will speak with one voice. We are firmly determined to do everything in our power to bring about the political union of Europe.

Interview of the Federal Chancellor with the Italian Newspaper "Corriere della Sera" on November 21, 1970 (Excerpt)

Question:

You once said that the frontiers between the EEC countries would have to be transformed into administrative lines in view of a political union. Would that not conflict with the Moscow Treaty? Do you not believe that the Soviet Union will contest a "Lesser Europe" solution?

Answer:

I have not got that impression. Rather, I am proceeding on the assumption that the Soviet Union recognizes that the European Community is a reality and is concerned to arrive at a realistic relationship with it. The German-Soviet Treaty does not, of course, impede the unification of Western Europe. The

Soviet Union has not made any influence of this kind felt; nor would we be able to allow her to do so. Those who are concerned in the European Community take the decisions about it; no one else.

Question:

You have said that the Atlantic Alliance and the policy towards Europe constitute the foundations of the Federal Government's policy towards the East. Sometimes ideas of a different tenor have been proclaimed about this. Do you think that the criticism of the opponents of the *Ostpolitik* is totally unfounded?

Answer:

I can understand that there are voices critical and sceptical of our *Ostpolitik*. Such voices are always to be heard whenever a new element makes its appearance in international policies. But there is no contradiction between our policy towards the West and Europe and our policy towards the East. The fact of the matter is that all European States are endeavouring to arrive at better relations with the East. For a long time the Federal Republic was last in the queue and was criticized for it because of this. At bottom, we are only doing what other countries started doing long before us because it was easier for them. By rendering our contribution, we are also, quite generally, supporting the efforts of others.

Speech of the Federal Minister of Economics, Prof. Dr. Karl Schiller, before the European Parliament in Strasbourg on November 18, 1970

Mr. President, Ladies and Gentlemen,

I believe that this is an important day for Europe and the Parliament of Europe. All speakers here have stressed that the economic and monetary union constitutes the central problem for further integration in Europe. Here the decision will be taken on the direction to be taken and the ground-line of the further economic and political development in Europe.

In point of fact, such a central problem has its place in the Parliamentary discussion, since we want, all of us, not only a technocratically governed Europe but at the same time we want, all of us, a Europe established on the basis of government by parliament. If any further evidence were needed of this, today's debate has certainly shown that the road to the economic and monetary union is impossible without the development of effective parliamentary control. This has been expressed very clearly in the Werner Report. I hope it will also be adopted by

the Council of Ministers when it starts discussing the document on the 23rd.

I would like to go quite briefly into some of the points brought up in the debate. In doing so, I will, as is customary in the second round, speak not only as President of the Council; I am doubtless also allowed to reply as a member of the Council and my country's representative.

With regard to the Werner Report as a whole, and as far as the attitude of the Council of Ministers is concerned, I would particularly like to reassure Mr. Deputy Löhr. The Council of Ministers has addressed itself to the task assigned it last December at the conference of the Heads of State and Government with great enthusiasm and great energy, and also with great haste. It started on the preparatory work last January and February and then approved very quickly certain aspects of the operations of the commission that was set up in March under Prime Minister Werner. As is well-known, this working group under Prime Minister Werner carried on its activity during the summer with great energy. At the end of May it submitted its interim report. Before you here had passed its interim report it had already submitted its final report, which has meanwhile become available—officially too—for debate in this Honourable House. I think, therefore, that the Council of Ministers in company with the Commission—Mr. Vice-President Barre has already referred to the historic process—has carried out its duty in bringing matters for decision, quickly and energetically, before the commencement of the first stage.

In today's debate, the question of the political content of the phased plan has been touched on several times. I believe I am able to say that the Council is certainly fully aware of the political significance of the economic and monetary union. I myself would like to go a stage further and say quite clearly that, in my view, a political union is not to be created in a vacuum, in a retort, but only on the foundation of the convergence of the material interests of the European countries. As long as we fail to bring about this convergence of the material interests of the European Member Countries, a political union is nothing but an illusion.

Without descending into alien imagery, here we need the firm substructure of the common economic interests and the common economic policy if we wish to make political headway too. The Werner Report itself now envisages very clearly political implications, political progress, in the individual stages as a condition of further economic development, as a precondition of a succession of further economic stages.

I believe that this combination is proper and realistic and that from stage to stage decisions will be taken not on the lines of unperceptive automation mechanically engendering this succession of stages from year to year but, as Mr. Vice-President Barre has said, with the assistance of the conclusions to be drawn from the previous stage. This is an eminently political gradation, an eminently political succession of steps, which, at the same time, as the Werner Plan has said, will be a ferment for the actual political union in Europe.

Now Mr. Deputy Löhr has asked: Will the Council of Ministers, with its eyes on the final stage, say exactly what economic union, what monetary union, is meant and sought? I can say that I believe the Council will do exactly that. But in doing so it must always say, if it sticks to the Werner Report, that from stage to stage there will be no taking of decisions automatically, either in the views of the Commission or in the report of the Werner group.

If you care to hear anything about the quality of the economic and monetary union, I must say that it must be an economic union and a monetary union distinguished by stability. And that is not merely a meaningless phrase but an eminently political —indeed a compelling— statement. If at the end of the initial stage the Commission makes its proposals on the strength of experiences, not to speak of—as is proposed in the Werner Report, and I think it is a good proposal—a Government conference on the experiences to date and the further steps to be taken on the road to the economic and monetary union, then it will also be a matter of deciding whether, in the three years, progress has been made in the direction of the stability of the Community or whether, in the three years, there has been any turning aside or slipping in the direction of more stability in Europe. Then that is also a highly political problem whether new conditions, new qualifications, are formulated for the next stage.

And something else on which, I think, we are all agreed: the parallelism between the aim and actions of economic policy and the convergencies in monetary policy. We must say farewell to the present system. We have a system of the Common Market. We have a customs union. But we have—and we all know it—a system of still-varying national economic, fiscal and market development policies. And such a system is for ever condemned to produce continually imbalances.

It is precisely because of this that the Council and the Commission have already developed, here and now, instruments for the better coordination of economic, fiscal and market development policies, but they will certainly maintain that, in the sense of the parallelism which, in the Werner Report, has a fundamental importance for the future and the succession of stages, similar progress in the convergence of the individual economic policies and in the merging of monetary policies is a condition, is necessary, and is inevitable.

With the commencement of the deliberations on the phased plan at the beginning of the year, it became clear to us quite quickly that, with imbalances arising, an abstract monetary machine for Europe without parallel convergence or harmonization of economic policy would break down very rapidly. Certainly under the circumstances prevailing in Europe in the '70s an entirely separate solution on the lines of a solely monetary union will not suffice. We need both; and I believe that in this the Council and the Commission and the authors of the Werner group report are in agreement.

In the views put forward by both—the Commission and the Werner group—reference has been made to the alliance between growth and stability. I believe that we shall also reach agreement on this point in the Council.

And now, to a special point—to the phased plan for the '70s and the States that are prepared to accede to the Community. I will not evade the problem that Mr. Cousté has raised here. I also believe that something must be said about it here and now.

I would like to propose the following solution to the problem. According to the Werner Report, and, I hope, according to the Council's decisions also, the first stage, particularly, which is to cover three years, is an experimental stage, a stage of pragmatic advance, a stage in which no decisions will be taken on concrete amendments to the Treaty and additional political necessities until the three years are up.

I believe that if, within this space of time, we and the countries prepared to accede are given the possibility to become acquainted with this succession of stages, they, and with them ourselves, will reach—as we all hope—a positive decision. With amendments to the Treaty that are necessary for the second or the medium stages, we ought, therefore, to wait until the end of the initial stage to make it possible for the applicant countries to acquire a knowledge of all these preparations and also to express their opinions about them, but then, nevertheless, to be able on their part to concur promptly in this succession of stages.

Another problem that has been touched on, if only on the fringe, is the question of the fixing or not of the time plan. I think that here the Werner Report and the views of the Commission are already quite clear. It is precisely because of the political aspects that we need a plan with a high degree of elasticity. For this reason the initial stage has rightly been fixed as the stage of experimentation to last for three years. But the period of time covered by the further stages cannot be laid down at the moment automatically. A decision on the time schedule ought to be taken at the end of the initial stage at the Government conference on the basis of the proposals of the Commission and the Council's preparations.

However, the political will of the States prepared to accede to agree to these further stages would have to be clear from the very beginning.

As far as we know, the reactions so far of the applicants for accession to the phased plan are entirely positive. Nor should we allow ourselves to be put off by public criticism of any kind. The applicants for accession have stated that basically they see no insuperable obstacles on the road to the economic and monetary union. Well, that is what I have to say about the questions of the candidates for accession and the question of the fixing of dates for the succession of stages.

If here there is talk of stages, we know that what has been submitted to us in the Werner Report is no phased plan laying down a fixed number of stages. What is certain is that there is an initial stage and that there is a final stage. As far as I see it, the initial stage, according to the Werner Report, is the stage of convergence, and already the stage of putting to the proof, because the national policies will have to be approximated, and already in the initial stage.

The second stage, or I would prefer to say, the medium stages are, from all we have seen here, the stages of transformation—that is, the stages of transformation from competencies in the national spheres to Community bodies. The final stage—in Paris we once called it the "Elysium" of Europe—is characterized by the transfer of all economic and fiscal policy powers to the Community. The transfer of monetary policy powers to a European central bank system is also characterized by the high symbolic value of a then standard European currency.

In my opinion we can reach this Elysium of the final stage—and only on the stages thereto do we make progress—only if in the first place we refrain from any automatics from the very beginning. In future, any progress after the initial stage will be possible only if political breaks are also introduced—that is, only if the transition from one phase to the others is accompanied by a political overhauling in the discussions.

And, secondly, progress in this succession of stages, or on this ladder of stages, towards the final stage is possible only if all economic, political and social aspects are considered at the same time and, so far as possible, frontally: that is to say, if from the transition from one stage to the others account is taken of the interdependence of all economic and political factors.

A third is necessary for us to reach this final stage. The monetary union, which we seek for the final stage, must for its part exist in a world monetary system which also finds itself in a state of change. Anyone who attended the last meeting of the International Monetary Fund this year at Copenhagen will have noticed that in the international monetary system too discussions are in progress to reform this international monetary system on the lines of greater elasticity. I believe that our European economic and monetary union of the future can exist and reach its actual goal only if from the outset it takes notice of those global worldwide tendencies of the reform of the international monetary system. Our European monetary union must then be governed by the principle of internal stability and external elasticity. That means price stability internally, but externally a certain common elasticity in the question of parity in exchange rates towards the outside. The day can come when a European hard currency bloc, if it has arisen out of the stability community, must perhaps improve its common parity vis-à-vis other currencies.

I can see the existence of this road only if we choose the road via a Europe of stability. In any case we shall reach the final stage, if at all, only if—and I say it again—we do not place the principle of stability at risk in the initial stage. The Europe of the future will be a Europe of stability or it will not be able to exist. A Europe with an ailing monetary policy can be no energetic and united Europe. The final stage, now seeming like Utopia, can be realized if in advance at all stages we do not abandon the basis of solidarity.

Announcement of the Foreign Office

On December 22, 1970, in Rome, Ambassador Rolf Lahr deposited with the Italian Government the German ratification documents of the Treaty of April 22, 1970, on the amendment of certain budgetary provisions in the Treaty on the establishment of the European Communities and those of the Treaty on the setting-up of a Joint Council and a Joint Commission of the European Communities. At the same time the Federal Republic of Germany's Deputy Permanent Representative, Ministerialdirigent Bömcke, handed the Council's Secretary-General the German document approving the Resolution of the Council of the European Communities, of April 1, 1970, on the replacement of the Member States' financial contributions by the Community's own funds.

With this, the Federal Republic of Germany has—so far as lies in her power—created the precondition that the aim that the Communities' budget can be covered out of the Communities' funds, fixed by the Heads of State and Government at the conference at The Hague, can be achieved by the time laid down.

The German Bundestag approved the terms of the Treaty on November 6, 1970. France has already deposited the documents; Luxembourg and Italy have approved the fiscal constitution. The process of approval is under way in the other Member Countries.

These new arrangements signify an important turning-point in the history of the European Communities. Through the fiscal autonomy transferred to them, the European Communities will at last be distinguished from the international organizations of a traditional character. As the Federal Chancellor emphasized in his major speech before the Bundestag on November 6, 1970, this fiscal autonomy is an element of an anticipated federative system.

The German Bundestag's unanimous approval of these important new arrangements is to be embedded in the five aims that, in pursuance of the Federal Chancellor's statements in the ratification debate, the Federal Government has set for this decade in particular:

- the early enlargement of the Community by the States prepared to accede;
- the establishment of the economic and monetary union which is to extend and complement the Treaties of Rome;
- the development of the emerging political co-operation in Western Europe in such a way as to enable it to result in a political community;
- the establishment of the partnership of the Community with America and the assumption of international political responsibility in an appropriate manner;
- the following of the possibilities existing at any particular time of communication and co-operation with the countries of Eastern Europe and the putting of them to account in the general interest.

In detail:

Own Revenue

Through the Resolution of April 21, 1970, the European Communities are, from January 1, 1971, assigned all revenues from the agricultural levies as well as a share, growing by January 1, 1975, to 100 per cent., of the customs revenues (whereby, however, 10 per cent. of the customs revenues will be refunded to the Member States as levying costs). In the interim period, from 1971 to 1974, the Member States have to make additional financial contributions for the overall financing of the Communities' budget in the following proportions:

Belgium	6.8 per cent.
Germany	32.9 per cent.
France	32.6 per cent.
Italy	20.2 per cent.
Luxembourg	0.2 per cent.
The Netherlands	7.3 per cent.

However, to avoid too great fluctuations, the annual changes in the contributions to be paid by the Member States in the period up to 1975 have upper and lower limits; accordingly, the share to be paid by each Member State must not be more than 1 per cent. above, and not more than 1.5 per cent. below, the amount paid in the previous year.

By 1974 the total payments of the Federal Government of Germany to the budget of the European Communities (levies, customs revenues and financial contributions) will amount to about 32.64 per cent.

From 1975 onwards, the whole of the Communities' budget will be financed out of its own funds, the finance still remaining covered by receipts from the value added tax. For this, each Member State pays the Communities an amount resulting from the application of a certain rate to a proportionment basis uniform for all Member States. This rate must amount to 1 per cent. at the most.

At the same time this maximum limit signifies a—dynamic—limitation of the revenues of the European Communities. According to present advance estimates, for 1975, besides the revenue from customs and agricultural levies, about 0.6 per cent. of the amount of the proportionment basis of the value added tax will cover the financial requirements unless important new tasks are undertaken by the European Communities. With the proportionment basis of the value added tax increasing annually by about 6 per cent., it is likely that the Communities will have an adequate margin in the following years as well.

However, in this stage too—holding good up to December, 1977—the share of each Member State must not amount to more than 2 per cent. or less than 2 per cent., in comparison with the previous year. From 1978 onwards, this limitation ceases to apply.

Strengthening of the Budgetary Powers of the European Parliament

To offset the growing financial autonomy of the European Communities, the element of democratic control will also be strengthened by the treaty of April 22, 1970, on amending certain budgetary provisions of the European Community treaties. To this end the budgetary powers of the European Parliament are also to be extended in two phases.

In the interim phase, lasting up to the end of 1974, the Council will continue to take the final decision regarding budgetary procedure; only by a qualified majority, however, will it reject proposals of the European Parliament for amendments which do not lead to additional expenditure. The Council has also undertaken not to amend the budgetary estimates for the expenditure of the European Parliament.

In the normal phase, from 1975 onwards, the final decision regarding the budgetary procedure will lie basically with the European Parliament. Thereby, however, the Parliament is bound by the material law set by the Council. The actual sphere of decision therefore extends merely to the administrative expenditure—i.e., the budgetary funds not already covered by the legal acts of the Council.

In a minute dated April 22, 1970, the Council has, however, undertaken to examine in detail proposals promised by the Commission for extending the rights of the Parliament.

Answer of the Federal Government to a Major Question of the Parliamentary SPD and FDP Parties with Reference to the Federal Government's Foreign Policy on January 21, 1971

For the Federal Government, the Major Question of the Parliamentary SPD and FDP Parties provides a welcome occasion for being able to give a comprehensive account to the German Bundestag and the German public after a year of foreign political activity. At the same time, in the report on the State of the Nation, the Federal Government will describe its efforts towards improving intra-German relations and the questions relating thereto.

The Federal Government has repeatedly emphasized that

- the assured and solid relationship of friendship with its Western partners, which comes to expression in the Alliance and in the European Community, is the foundation of its foreign policy,

- it seeks to strengthen further the links and the co-operation with the nations and States in the West,

- it is interested, in the interest of our fellow-countrymen in the other part of Germany also, in improving relations with Eastern Europe, in understanding and a settlement,

- it is prepared to take into account the growing responsibility of the Federal Republic and Europe towards the problems of the Third World.

"Continuity and Renewal" were the guiding principles enunciated in the Government Policy Statement made by the Federal Chancellor before the German Bundestag on October 28, 1969. These principles still apply. Thereby, the Federal Government seeks to develop further the tried and tested traditions and at the same time to measure up to the demands of a rapidly changing world.

The foreign policy of the Federal Republic of Germany is planned on a long-term basis.

The Federal Government is aware that use must be made of every possibility offered for preserving peace.

The following are the answers to the individual questions:

Question 1

To what extent has it been possible to combine the deepening and enlargement of the European Communities, decided on at the summit conference at The Hague, with increasing political co-operation of the States of Western Europe?

Answer

The long-term aim of the Resolutions adopted at the summit conference at The Hague is the political unification of Europe.

The immediate tasks posed by the Heads of State and Government at The Hague for the operations within the Communities have been fulfilled in 1970 to a gratifying extent.

- The Council adopted the Resolution on the creation of the European Communities' own revenue; after ratification by the Member Countries the Resolution entered into force on January 1, 1971.

- The arrangements concerning the European Parliament's budgetary powers included in the Community Treaties were improved by an amendment to the Treaties; after approval by the national Parliaments, this amendment entered into effect on January 1, 1971.

- Negotiations on entry were initiated with Denmark, the United Kingdom, Ireland and Norway. Talks have opened on the regulation of the relationship with those EFTA countries which are not acceding.

- The Council agreed on the new functions of the European Social Fund, thereby opening the way towards making it a dynamic instrument of a European forward-looking employment policy.
- The Council passed the Ordinance on the financing of the common agricultural policy.
- The restructuring of EURATOM's Joint Research Centre was approved; important progress has thereby been achieved in the sphere of EURATOM.
- The Council approved additional market regulations for wine, tobacco, fish and textile fibres.

With this, the following has been achieved:

The completion of the Common Market is effected with the conclusion of the transitional phase; the negotiations on the enlargement of the Community have advanced earlier than expected from the stage of the mere establishment of facts, and have since made good progress.

The further deepening of the Community is especially assisted by the planned economic and monetary union. Although it proved impossible to achieve the aim first set—the commencement of the initial phase by January 1, 1971—important preparatory work has been accomplished with the Werner Report; extensive agreement has been reached in the Council of Ministers of the European Community on many individual questions. The aim remains to set in operation as soon as possible the phased plan for the realization of an economic and monetary union in this decade. Here too it is a matter of exploiting the great potential of the European Communities in the general interest and thereby promoting closer association in Europe.

These efforts are accompanied by the extension and improvement of co-operation among the Member States, approved at The Hague, in the sphere of foreign policy. The Federal Government regards this as being of crucial importance for the future of Europe. A mechanism of qualified foreign political consultations, with the candidates for accession participating, has in the meantime been created.

In the light of the efforts towards intensified co-operation, the Federal Government, in its Memorandum of November 18, 1970, proposed to the other Member States of the European Communities consultations before the commencement of any new international technological co-operation and, above all, negotiations in international organizations or bodies, should fundamental questions of the policy towards science be affected. The purpose of these consultations is to proceed from the supplying of information to discussion on the common aims and to arrive as quickly as possible at the necessary coordination of attitudes.

With this, the forward-looking decisions of the conference at The Hague are therefore being implemented step by step. Mutual confidence is being strengthened. European solidarity is being revived. Clear perspectives for the European policy of the '70s have been developed. Based on the institutionally secured system of the European Community, a priority aim of European policy is to develop and improve the co-operation and to deepen the awareness of common interests.

With the strengthening and the supporting of this co-operation in Western Europe, the Federal Government is continuing a policy that has been approved by the vast majority of the population ever since the Federal Republic was created. If as a result of this international co-operation, a growing number of nations shares in the prosperity, the prospects of a world at peace are improved.

Question 2

How does the Federal Government judge the existing political co-operation of the States of the European Communities and the political partnership in NATO?

Answer

1. Co-operation in the European Communities

The Federal Government does not regard the existing foreign political co-operation of the States of the European Communities as yet being adequate. Nevertheless, a practical start promising of success has been made with the foreign political consultations of the Six.

Progress towards European union has suffered for a long time because there was nothing in the political sphere to compare with the economic integration. However, the summit conference at The Hague, on December 1 and 2, 1969, brought considerable progress. The Foreign Ministers of the six European Community countries were commissioned to examine "how in the perspective of the enlargement" the European Communities "progress could best be achieved in the area of political unification". This foreign political co-operation was initiated with the "Report of the Foreign Ministers to the Heads of State and Government of the Member States of the European Communities", passed to time on October 27, 1970, at Luxembourg; a sort of "phased plan" for the political unification of Europe constitutes the first stage of this unification. There is to be a review of what has been achieved after two years at the latest.

In the meantime, in a good atmosphere of understanding, the first consultations of the Six took place on November 19, 1970, in Munich and the first exchange of views among the Ten—i.e., the Six and the four countries prepared to accede—on December 2 in Brussels. The European Parliament and the Commission of the European Communities will actively participate in these joint activities.

A multi-stage consultation mechanism is envisaged for the foreign political co-operation of the Six. In the first place there is to be no categoric institutionalization. However, the rudiments of this are offered by the Political Committee and the stipulation that each Foreign Ministry concerned nominates a conversation partner for the co-operation. These conversation partners remain in close contact with one another. The Political Committee has already convened several times. With these meetings it has been seen that all concerned are determined to achieve a constructive co-operation.

In the meantime, the constant routine co-operation of the six Foreign Ministers, also envisaged in the Report, has started. The supplying of information on important foreign political events is being carried on not only bilaterally. In each case the representatives of the embassies of the other five European Community countries are informed together on the spot.

Beyond the stipulations in the Report, the Foreign Ministers have intensified the foreign political co-operation. An identical instruction laying down the procedure for close co-operation at diplomatic level has been sent to the diplomatic representatives of the six European Community countries in Third Countries and with international organizations.

To sum up: It can be said that promising experience has been made with the new method of co-operation. The Luxembourg Report is an important step on the difficult road to a comprehensive union of Europe—a Europe which, as it says in the communiqué of The Hague, "is able to assume its responsibility in the world of tomorrow and to make the contribution that is appropriate to its tradition and its mission".

In the opinion of the Federal Government, this development process, the tempo of which will not, of course, be determined by the Germans alone, is to result in a common European policy.

Announcement of the Press and Information Office of the Federal Government

The Federal Government welcomes the agreement reached on February 9, 1971, in the Council of Ministers of the European Community on the gradual realization of an economic and monetary union in the course of the next ten years.

With this Resolution another crucial part of the task set by the Heads of State and Government in December, 1969, has been accomplished. With the economic and monetary union, the European Community takes on an added quality. In the course of the process, new powers and responsibilities, subject to parliamentary control at Community level, will gradually be transferred to the Community.

In the general view of all Member States, the Community is to become a community of stability and growth and will increase its contribution to the international division of labour.

For the organization of the Community in the final stage, important principles have already been laid down in the light of which, with the transition to the second stage, decisions will be taken on the further course to be adopted until the economic and monetary union has been realized.

In this connection, in the interest of the policy of stability, special importance attaches to ensuring that the progress made in economic policy is similar to that made in monetary policy. The necessary arrangements have been concerted to achieve this parallelism.

The establishment of an economic and monetary union is not only a process of great political significance but also a decisive step forward on the road to the integration of Europe. The Federal Government takes satisfaction in stating that, in accordance with the directives contained in the Werner Report, in Brussels all Member States helped to create the preconditions whereby the union will be a more harmonious and logical development of the Common Market.

Statement of the Federal Minister of Economics, Prof. Dr. Karl Schiller, on February 10, 1971, at an Informative Gathering in Bonn on the Meeting of the Council of Ministers of the European Communities on February 8 and 9, 1971, in Brussels

Yesterday's decision represents a turning-point of moment. Yesterday an important breakthrough was achieved, or, as the French have written today in Paris: "Europe sets out on the journey". Yesterday we formulated a goal that can perhaps best be described so: Europe as an economic and monetary union will be a community of stability and growth open to the world. Importance is also attached in some formulations to a sequence—first of all stability, then growth.

Yesterday's discussion took place in an exceptionally friendly atmosphere and everyone was at pains to display the necessary readiness for compromise.

Since December 14 and 15, when we found ourselves in a certain confrontation, talks and soundings have been going on between Paris and Bonn in the course of the Franco-German consultations as also between Rome and Paris and with the Commission. All these preparatory talks and soundings well prepared the compromise that was found yesterday. Yesterday the so-oft-invoked "spirit of The Hague" was present, something which has not always been the case.

At the conclusion of these soundings and preparatory talks, I was able, on January 29, to outline in the German Bundestag, in the name of the Federal Government, our line of negotiation for the round in Brussels yesterday and the day before; it had partly resulted from these preparatory talks, although also from our own ideas of the objectives and our assessment of the situation. If I compare these eight points with what was achieved yesterday, it is seen that there is almost total agreement.

1.   Our first thesis was that the initial stage of this phased plan was no goal in itself. The political will to proceed to the transition to the further stages and to the completion of the economic and monetary union would also have to be expressed. Now, since yesterday it has been officially stated in Brussels, and I quote:

> "The Council and the representatives of the Member States proclaim their political will to create in the course of the next ten years an economic and monetary union in accordance with a phased plan starting to operate on January 1, 1971."

You see that there has been adherence to the old date, January 1, 1971, after the tradition already exercised in Brussels in former cases to stop the clock.

2.   Secondly, in the Bundestag we stated the desire to ensure an effective parallelism between the monetary policy union and the economic policy union. In Brussels it now says, and I quote:

> "The creation of the currency union will have to be accompanied by, in particular, parallel progress in the convergence and subsequent standardization of the economic policies."

3.   Thirdly, we have said that the final stage must not get lost in any remote European fog,

there to vanish finally altogether, but that we would have to lay down certain basic principles for the final stage without, however, anticipating in a perfectionist fashion all detailed arrangements for the final stage. In point of fact we have been able to define, for the final stage, the organizational requirements, the necessary transfer of powers, and the further institutional development.

4.   In this connection—and this is the fourth point—a particular part is played by the question as to what is to become of the Community organs. We have said that these must now be placed in a position whereby they can exercise their powers quickly and effectively, that parliamentary control is necessary. Now, in Brussels, it has been decided, and I quote:

> "The institutions of the Community will be placed in a position to exercise their economic and fiscal policy responsibility quickly and effectively.

> "The Community policies laid down within the framework of the economic and monetary union are subject to the deliberations and the control of the European Parliament."

This version, that those measures the Community will institute in future within the framework of the economic and monetary union are to be subject to the deliberations and the control of the European Parliament, was the maximum that we, especially the Netherlands and the Federal Republic, were able to get out of our French friends, whose ideas, particularly in relation to the European Parliament, are naturally somewhat different from ours, even if we have already indicated our agreement with this formulation.

5.   Fifthly, we said in the Bundestag that, in view of the various ideas of our central banks, we now had to ensure a certain central bank policy on our own responsibility for a European central bank system. We ourselves take the

view that an independent European central bank system could be an outstanding model with autonomy, even for the future common monetary policy to be pursued in the final phase. Now, the Brussels Resolution says, and I quote:

"Within the framework of its own responsibility, the Community's central bank system contributes to the realization of the Community's aims of stability and growth."

In addition, there is another Resolution, adopted by the Council, with which the governors of the central banks are invited themselves to lay down, in consultation with one another, the modalities.

6. Sixthly, we said that it would have to be ensured that, at the end of the initial stage, legally binding decisions were taken for the transition from the initial stage and that in this connection measures amending or supplementing the Treaty—and for this there are, as is well-known, various Articles in the Treaty—must be agreed and, moreover, up to the completion.

In Brussels the Council's common Declaration of Intent was formulated to the effect that measures for the full realization of the economic and monetary union must be laid down before the conclusion of the initial stage. Then follow three categories—which we had already been able to discuss to a certain extent with our friends in Paris, in the sense of an exchange of views and not in the sense of joint decisions. These three categories concern decisions taken within the framework of the existing Treaty, decisions pursuant to Article 235—that is, through supplementing the Treaty according to a certain procedure—and, finally, also of amendments to the Treaty according to procedures outlined in Article 286.

In this way we succeeded in securing the agreement of our French partner that for the decisions to be taken at the conclusion of the initial stage amendments to the Treaty would be envisaged—something that it was certainly impossible to achieve on December 14 and 15 last.

7. Then, as the seventh point, in the Bundestag we expressed the view that, in order to ensure that the development of the economic and monetary measures would, actually and effectively, run parallel an expiration clause ought to be included. This would mean that if, after a certain time, the economic policy measures were not running parallel to the monetary policy measures, the monetary policy measures would lapse at a certain date.

In Brussels we have now also discussed this "clause de prudence", as M. Pompidou called it when I put it forward in Paris in a number of variants. After a very lively debate it was agreed by everybody. The period over which these monetary measures are to run is thereby limited to five years. This present year was, as is usual at the conference table, our concession. In the matter itself, in the substance, we have secured the full acceptance of the "clause de prudence". For us, this is of particular significance, since what takes place economically, in economic policy, in the initial stage, consists, in essence, in the Community, of the Council giving aids for the orientation of economic and fiscal policy to the Member State bodies in order to bring the individual policy measures into closer alignment. All this is the intention for the initial stage.

Where something really legally binding takes place is in the sphere of monetary policy. In the initial stage the central banks will together undertake interventions in the foreign currency markets. Possibly a Reserve and Foreign Currency Offset Fund will be instituted in the first stage. Through the interventions the band widths will be narrowed or extended within the framework of the International Monetary Fund. All in all, those are the three or four groups of measures planned for the initial stage.

We considered that if by the end of the initial stage corresponding measures had not put in an appearance in the sphere of economic policy, these monetary policy measures would remain as a torso of the entire economic and monetary union but would then cease to operate, whereby it is not our intention that this entire process would go back to square one, to January 1, 1971. Instead, our intention is, by fixing this date, to exert a healthy pressure, so that at the end of the initial stage decisions for the correction of economic policy can be taken.

8. Eighthly, we also said, finally, in the Bundestag, that the Resolutions must be so formulated that the candidate countries—the United Kingdom, Denmark, Ireland and Norway—would be able to take an option at the conclusion of the initial stage. This has clearly been achieved. It has also been talked about that at the conclusion of the initial stage, when the actual legally binding decisions in the economic and fiscal spheres are to be taken, we shall possibly be able to welcome a larger number of members. There is no doubt that even in this respect our "*clause de prudence*"—there was no express mention of it in the discussion itself—is adequate.

Therefore, we were successful in Brussels in making the line of compromise we had imagined prevail. In point of fact we have not surrendered anything fundamental, but the vital elements, the principles as set out in exemplary fashion and very clearly in the Werner Report, have been preserved.

On the way now secured the process towards the economic and monetary union can now be followed without any dangerous list towards the monetary policy side.

Nor do we want to decide on such an uncontrolled automation in the development such as we are confronted by in, for instance, the European agricultural market regulations, about which no one, not even the farmers, are happy and which, because of the inherent force in this apparatus, can only with difficulty be corrected.

With regard to this new version of the decision, it has often been said that with this phased plan we—like our French friends—are pursuing a pragmatic line. I would say that there certainly is a pragmatic element in the initial stage, but it is a pragmatism for a limited period, a pragmatism with a firm goal, for, particularly, the final stage.

That, in essence, is the result of the consultations of last Monday and Tuesday. It certainly does not mean that we have anticipated all the working group under Prime Minister Werner set us in its report last year, but what could be achieved under the present circumstances was in fact yesterday achieved—more, indeed, than anyone had previously thought possible.

Moreover, it is also clear to us that the decisions do not cover the whole of the ten years, over the whole period up to 1980, but that the next important junction and final decision will come at the conclusion of the initial stage in the categories I have already described, namely, the decision on the necessary supplementation, demanded of us, of the experiences we have gained up to then in the sphere of monetary policy by corresponding safeguards in the sphere of economic policy.

In the coming days and weeks there will be a pretty deep discussion on what has, and what has not, been achieved and on what is to be expected in the coming period for the further development of Europe. We are naturally very gratified that we have now succeeded in arriving at an agreement.

This doubtless also documents sufficiently—and particularly with regard to the special role the Federal Republic has played this last year within the Werner Group and in the Council—that, within the framework of our overall policy towards the outside, we have made headway, in the staunchest way possible, in our policy towards the West and our policy towards integration.

Speech of the Federal Chancellor before the Members of the Monnet Committee in Bonn on February 23, 1971

I. It gives me great pleasure to welcome you here and to express my pleasure that the Action Committee—under the chairmanship of the highly respected President, Jean Monnet—has come to Bonn for its deliberations.

For Europe, this is a particularly important year: it is hoped that it will be possible to conclude the negotiations on the enlargement of the Community. The transition to the economic and monetary union has been initiated. The political co-operation has commenced.

The Government of the Federal Republic of Germany has not allowed itself—and I can say this without exaggeration—to be found wanting in initiatives and efforts of its own. We are proceeding on the assumption that it will be possible in this decade to bring about the vital changes that were initiated with the summit conference at The Hague. Without wishing to anticipate your deliberations, may I make the following remarks about some of the topical questions.

It should be possible in the next few months to take decisions regarding the accession of the United Kingdom and the further enlargement of the Community. This will provide fresh opportunities for all concerned. I do not belittle the significance of the financial arrangements that still have to be negotiated. Here a realistic compromise must be found.

With the development of the economic and monetary union the Community will acquire a new dynamism. It will depend very much on whether—when things have advanced far enough—the hurdle from the initial stage to the second can be taken. We regard the "prudence clause" the Council of Ministers has agreed as primarily a measure to stimulate the indispensable parallelism between progress in economic and monetary policies.

For the political co-operation, the Foreign Ministers' Luxembourg report signified a modest, if concrete, beginning. I am confident that we shall make progress in this way and that we shall be able to render our own European contribution towards, for instance, solving the dangerous problems in the Middle East and the Central Mediterranean area and meet our international political responsibility better than hitherto.

Let me immediately add what I earlier pointed out: in this stage of the development in Western Europe special importance attaches to trusting relations with the United States. First and foremost, in the matter of commercial policy, the most satisfactory balancing of interests, which diverge from the very nature of things in individual questions, must be found. The readjustment of interests demands a reliable and systematic dialogue.

II. Here and there voices have been heard proclaiming fears that we in the Federal Republic of Germany might, via our *Ostpolitik*, be neglecting the aims we have set ourselves in the West and, above all, in Western Europe. The facts contradict such fears. In spite of this I would like, before you, once more to point out the following connections.

In the first place, we are aware that our efforts towards reaching an understanding and a settlement with our Eastern neighbours can meet with success only if, at the same time, co-operation and solidarity in Western Europe are deepened, extended and improved.

Secondly, together with our Western partners we have exhaustively discussed all steps serving détente. Our policy is not only "rooted"; it is an element in the common orientation of the Western Alliance we have helped to develop.

Thirdly, from this it follows that there can be no doubt about the priorities. Upborne by the "policy towards the West", we are concerned to make our specific contribution towards reducing tensions and slowly preparing a peace order for the continent of Europe.

Years ago this Committee was already pointing out the need to initiate a new phase of communication and co-operation between Western and Eastern Europe. It is, in fact, important that our Community should appear as a partner worthy of trust in the eyes of our Eastern neighbours as well. Not only must we bring about that the Soviet Union and her partners in Eastern Europe recognize the Community as a new unit with powers of its own; they must themselves be able to realize that their own interests call for a satisfactory relationship with the Community.

I myself expect that within this decade the Community will become the socially most progressive large region in the world.

My hope, notwithstanding the various forms taken by the social systems, goes beyond this—to a "Europe of co-operation".

With all frankness I add: For us Germans, this is the only framework within which we can alleviate, reduce, and also one day overcome, the cleavage of our nation. There are no isolated answers to the questions exercising our minds. We know that we are in duty bound dedicated to peace, and we wish to relieve our neighbours of unnecessary cares. This leads us not only to resignation but also to increased commitment to Europe.

III. Perhaps I may be allowed to make some other remarks about the final form of European union. The discussion about this has been stimulated by what the French President said last month at his Press conference and by what the British Prime Minister stated recently before the conference of European parliamentarians.

When I recall the—at times rather too abstract—conflict of opinions in which the federalists and the confederalists have been embroiled in recent years, it seems to me that it is possible to detect a deeper contemplation of the actual goal. However limited the competencies—and perhaps in this connection the experiences we in the Federal Republic have gained with the instrument of "concurrent legislation" that is rooted in our Constitution might be advanced—clearly the goal is nevertheless a sensibly organized European Government able to take the necessary decisions in the spheres of common policy and subject to parliamentary control.

The discussion about the road leading to this seems, to me, to have become easier. Certainly it will take some time to arrive gradually at a solution acceptable to all partners. All the more should we in the meantime concentrate on the concrete steps it is possible at any time to take.

In the light of this, I wish your meeting a successful course, with results that stimulate the development.

Toast Given by the Federal Chancellor at the Dinner in Honour of the British Prime Minister, the Rt. Hon. Edward Heath, M.B.E., M.P., on April 5, 1971, at the Königshof Hotel, Bonn

Prime Minister, Ladies and Gentlemen,

It gives me very great pleasure, Prime Minister, to be able to welcome you and your attendants here tonight.

Last year we saw you here in Bonn as Leader of the Opposition. Today you are here with us as British Prime Minister. We are con-

scious of the honour you have done us in making your first journey abroad in the capacity of Head of Government to the Federal Republic of Germany.

Your visit takes place at a time in which important developments are taking place within the framework of European co-operation and important decisions in relation to the enlargement of the European Community are pending. Therefore this theme also stands well to the fore in our discussions, which are marked by a friendly and trusting spirit. The Federal Government is aware that, now that, in implementation of the decisions taken at The Hague in December, 1969, the twelve-year period of transition has been concluded, the system of our own revenues has been superseded, the political co-operation has been initiated, and the project of an economic and monetary union has been given a fair start, greater efforts must now be undertaken in order to bring the negotiations on the enlargement to a successful conclusion. It is necessary to find solutions which are in accordance both with the possibilities and the wishes of your country and with the interests of the Community. You may be sure that everything that lies in the Federal Government's power to bring about a happy solution will be done.

The United Kingdom may be certain that she is welcomed by the European Community. In this connection I am thinking not only of the gain the British potential in economy and technology, in skilled labour and international experience, will bring the Community. I am also thinking of the other qualities distinguishing your country and her people: the firmly rooted democratic tradition, a tolerance that does not exclude steadfastness, the capacity to master new problems and through evolutionary channels, and to combine expediently the old with the new. It is good if Britain does not keep these qualities merely to herself but exerts them in the Community for the good of all.

Here in the Federal Republic we fully understand that the question of accession is being discussed at great length, and even controversially, in your country. This demonstrates that the bond across the Channel has a historically crucial significance.

Among the present Member States of the Community there were also at the outset doubts whether the road on which we were embarking with the Treaties of Rome was the right one. But it is illuminating to state that the vast majority of the people in the six Member States view the Community and its further development in a positive light. I am confident that this will also be the case in your country when, after the natural initial difficulties of adaptation, the advantages for all concerned become evident.

We are at one in thinking that co-operation in Western Europe must be more than merely a means all the better to satisfy the needs of its inhabitants. We are also at one in thinking that the Community must not be looked upon as— as you say in Britain—a "closed shop" cutting itself off from the rest of the world. It must be open to the world. It must make its contribution towards increasing world trade. It must, in particular, in its relationship with the United States, but also with others, proclaim its preparedness to shoulder part of the international political responsibility.

Prime Minister, in your recent address before the conference in London of European parliamentarians you expressed this in words with which I can fully agree.

The closest possible co-operation of the nations of Western Europe is also necessary if we are to succeed in our efforts towards détente, in order in this way to alleviate the cleavage of Europe and, we hope, to be able one day to overcome it. This includes not only that—via the understanding in the Atlantic Alliance—we succeed in achieving a harmonization of our policies in Western Europe. It also includes that the individual partners consult one another as closely as possible about their bilateral projects. Prime Minister, of this the talks we have had about this theme are a good example.

Interview of the Federal Minister for Foreign Affairs, Walter Scheel, with the "Frankfurter Rundschau" of May 3, 1971 (Excerpt)

Question:

Have you not got the impression that the Federal Government's policy towards Western Europe has been given rather a back seat in favour of the policy towards the East?

Answer:

No, not in the very least. If anyone should have got this false impression, it is doubtless merely because polemic criticism of the policy towards the East is distracting attention from the results in the West and these—observed by themselves—are of a really sensational character. Therefore, polemics in the case of the policy towards the East does damage to the policy towards the West.

I hardly need to repeat that the Federal Government regards policy towards the East and policy towards the West as forming an inseparable whole. I hardly need to remind that right at the beginning of the work of this Federal Government stood the directives of the summit conference at The Hague. I would like, quite unemotionally, to mention some of the results.

1. In the Sphere of the Communities:

Completion of the customs union. Decision about fiscal constitution and the Community's own revenues. Opening of the negotiations on accession. Decision on EURATOM's Joint Research Centre. Commencement of the political co-operation of the Six. Decision on the development of the economic and monetary union.

2. In the Sphere of the Alliance:

Formation of the Europeans to a group within NATO. Unprecedented decision on a programme for strengthening Europe, adopted with appreciable German participation. Further development of the Alliance to form an instrument serving not only defence, but also giving new impulses towards détente. In the course of this development the Europeans in the Alliance acquire a new awareness of their responsibility.

Contribution of the Federal Chancellor to the "Bulletin" of May 6, 1971, on the Theme "A Forum of European Unity"

May 5, which is celebrated everywhere in the Member States of the Council of Europe as "Europe Day", provides an occasion for drawing up a balance of the development in Europe. For us Germans, this day has a special significance because it is twenty years, almost exactly to the day, since the Federal Republic officially became a member of the Council of Europe. As is well-known, the Council of Europe, in Strasbourg, was the first international organization to admit the Federal Republic as a partner with equal status.

For us Germans, the Council of Europe was an opportunity at a relatively early point of time to resume contact with the parliamentarians and representatives of the other European countries and so facilitate Germany's reappearance on the stage of international politics. Germany actively assisted in making the Council of Europe a forum in which fresh life was put into the European ideal. Here I would like—and at the same time as representative for others—only call to mind our friend Fritz Erler, who died far too early and to whom it is due, together with others, that the Council of Europe was able to render important services.

The practical results are worthy of notice. In dogged, minute work it has been possible to draw attention to the relative insignificance of national frontiers and to facilitate tourist travel beyond them. In the social and cultural spheres there has been pioneering work which has found expression in more than 60 European conventions and agreements. The most important of these is doubtless the European Convention on the Protection of Human Rights and Fundamental Freedoms, to which the Federal Republic of Germany acceded and as one of the first States to do so.

However, in spite of the numerous individual successes on the road towards rapprochement and the harmonization of legislation and law in many spheres, it cannot be forgotten that many of the hopes tied up with the founding of the Council of Europe more than twenty years ago have been disappointed. To many, the road to Europe is too slow, and particularly among the younger generation it is felt that willingness and ability, ideal and reality, are often still a long way from each other.

Exactly two years ago today, on the occasion of the celebration in London of the twentieth anniversary of the founding of the Council of Europe, I, as German Minister for Foreign Affairs and officiating Chairman of the Council of Europe's Ministerial Committee, recalled that "Strasbourg" was the starting-point for the closer co-operation of a number of our countries and pointed out that for the grandeur of the project that is called Europe we need a healthy mixture of belief in the future and sober realism.

Since then, much that is decisive has been achieved, particularly in the Europe of the Six.

The summit conference at The Hague put an end to the stagnation in the European Community. With the decisions on the financial arrangements and the economic and monetary union, the internal development of the Community entered a new, dynamic phase. The transfer of budgetary rights to the European Parliament is a step towards the democratization of the Community we seek. The Foreign Ministers' conference in Munich last November has led to an intensification of the political co-operation. We have every reason for not belittling these successes; they justify our gazing with confidence towards the future development.

Of crucial importance for the future of Europe is that, parallel to the internal development, it has been possible to embark upon the enlargement of the Community by the four countries seeking entry.

We in the Federal Republic have always proceeded on the assumption that the enlargement of the Community is as essential politically as it is economically, and that beyond its value for those directly concerned it also serves the interests of a greater Europe. Together with our partners we share the conviction that the enlargement of the Community is also necessary in order to assure Europe its proper place in the world. A Europe united on a broader basis would be an element of stability and would be able to render a valuable contribution towards the preservation of peace and the promotion of prosperity in the world.

The Council of Europe is Europe's most comprehensive alliance. Although its seventeen Member States belong to various groupings, or are non-committed or neutral, they have nevertheless associated themselves, on the strength of common ideals and convictions, for common action. The inherent opportunities should be utilized for strengthening co-operation. Here I am also thinking of the possibilities of a more extensive co-operation with other countries. Already States which are not members are co-operating in numerous projects, and the Council of Europe has concerned itself in recent years with inspiring the countries of Eastern Europe also to co-operate in areas in which this is possible.

The Council of Europe could be a bridge between the East and the West of our continent and help to lower barriers that divide. Herein lies a rewarding task and a complementation of other efforts towards détente, agreement and co-operation.

Statement of the Federal Chancellor on May 9, 1971, on both Television Programmes, on the Occasion of the Decision to Allow the Rate of Exchange of the D-Mark to Float

You have all been witnesses in these days of the struggle to maintain the stability of our currency. You will also have sensed what an uphill work it is to emerge from this struggle successfully.

It has once again become clear that for us there is no island of stability, yet there must be no doubt that we shall do everything in our power to achieve greater stability.

The Federal Government is just as little responsible for the immense inflows of dollars as it is for the rises in price, which are higher in almost all countries than with us. But it is the duty of the Federal Government to do what it is convinced it is now necessary to do in the interest of our country.

We shall now allow the exchange rate of the Mark to float for a time. This means for the time being a drop in the exchange rate of foreign currencies; this will not only put a brake on the inflow of foreign money but also make imports cheaper. An upward revaluation is not contemplated. We shall also put in hand a programme for stabilizing the domestic economy. The prime purpose of these measures is to check the tendency for prices to rise. This is causing us all anxiety, because every one of us sees that excessive rises in price lead to social injustices, that they prejudice the capacity of our economy to compete, that they bring high wage demands in their train, and that they curtail too much the public investments of the Federation, the *Länder* and the communes that are important for our common future. One important reason for these rises in price is the great influx of money from abroad. Although this is proof of the confidence in the value of the Mark and the productive power of our economy, this influx of money lessens the possibilities of the Federal Government and the Federal Bank to keep the market development under control. It was therefore necessary to do something to counteract this.

Of course we remain aware of our European responsibility, but extravagant rises in price are no suitable expression of European unity.

Up to now our good economic development has taken care that, despite rises in price, the real incomes of most persons have continued to increase. But this development is no security against the danger of our having to face economic setbacks. The Federal Government wishes to avoid such a danger and has therefore had recourse to extraordinary measures. However, let me add at the same time that we are decisively dependent on the understanding and co-operation of the large social groups.

I would like to express my particular thanks to Ministers Scheel and Schiller for the result they achieved at the latest meeting in Brussels. They succeeded in gaining the understanding of our partners that the present situation demands radical measures of the Federal Government.

On this understanding—that we ourselves have often shown towards others—we are also dependent when on Tuesday the Ministers of

Agriculture have to decide on special arrangements for our agriculture, whose revenues can be reduced as a result of fluctuations in the exchange rate of the Mark. The Federal Government considers it its obvious duty to assist the German farmers in this situation.

I know that certain sectors of our commerce and industry will be temporarily affected by our decisions, but I also know that our prosperity is based on the achievements of industry, on the employees' creative power, and on the spirit of enterprise. I would like, therefore, to assure everybody that I shall also take these aspects fully into account when making future decisions. You may be sure that the Federal Government is keeping in mind the good of all.

Contribution of the Federal Minister for Foreign Affairs, Walter Scheel, to the May, 1971, Edition of the Periodical "Aussenpolitik" on the Theme "Partial Balance of German Foreign Policy" (Excerpt)

I. The balance that has developed in Europe since the end of the Second World War has not resulted from European strength. Rather, it has been based on the balance of power between the two World Powers—the United States and the Soviet Union. At the same time, the ideological, political and social incompatibility of the two systems divides Europe and Germany.

This balance, which has been existing for 25 years, is mainly based on mutual deterrence. A set of rules of behaviour from bloc to bloc, from NATO State to Warsaw Pact State, is recognizable only in rough outlines. The feeling has become widespread among the international public that the "era of negotiations" has opened. This course has been embarked upon but it is wearisome. Time and again the question has been posed: Is it better to stabilize the existing balance by delimitation of the blocs among each other or by a limited co-operation among the partners to the Alliance and between State and State?

The West has chosen the latter way as it is the more natural, since

- in the first place, isolation increases tensions because it perpetuates the causes of tensions,
- secondly, below the threshold of the antagonisms there exist adequate starting points for a fragmentary identity of interests from bloc to bloc. Here I mean, in particular, the economic, cultural and technological spheres. These partial harmonies in the spheres of interest justify an exchange, and

- thirdly, peace will be more assured if efforts towards détente are added to the deterrence. Security through détente is the complementation of security through defence and not the other way round. Nevertheless, détente can be achieved only by extended intercourse between States.

If these ideas are correct—and they are shared by the Governments of all Western countries, if not by all the fluctuating bodies of public opinion—, the Federal Republic is confronted by the following question: How must she behave if she wishes to conform to the international model? As a medium industrial power, as one of the two States in Germany, the Federal Republic is not strong enough by herself to bring about détente, and yet, because of her peculiar position on the line of tension between the two blocs, she could be responsible for jeopardizing peace if she did not behave in conformity with the system. For this reason, the system of détente sought by the Governments places restrictions on the Federal Republic on the one hand but a special responsibility on the other. She has to be particularly cautious in developing her foreign relations. Above all, she has to avoid anything that could in fact prejudice the rights and responsibilities of the four Victor Powers for Berlin and Germany as a whole, because this would affect the basis of stability in Europe. Nor, in addition, should the Federal Republic allow herself to be guided by fictitious political standards—in other words, to claim for herself an identity which, objectively observed, she does not possess.

The Federal Government, to which I belong, is trying to develop such a policy. To us, it seems better to render a contribution towards European stability within the 1971 frontiers rather than to indulge in dreams about the 1937 frontiers. In a painful political process of experience, the "short road" to the reunification of our country has proved impracticable. We must set out on the "long road". It is necessary to organize a modus vivendi in Europe on the basis of facts . . .

II. What is the substance of the policy pursued by the Federal Government as a contribution towards the stabilization of security in Europe doing justice to the system?

1. Western Europe could achieve much in international politics if it spoke with one voice. The downfall of Europe was a result of nationalistic over-enthusiasm that disturbed the balance and finally destroyed it. To pursue the goal of European unity is a demand of the dynamic preservation of peace.

Starting from the conference at The Hague in December, 1969, our own political efforts are planned so systematically and with a regard for timing that priority is given to this goal. Since then we have achieved the following:

(a) On November 19, 1970, a conference of the Foreign Ministers of the six States of the European Community concerned itself for the first time with non-European political issues. A con-sultation mechanism was developed with the object of coordinating the six countries' foreign policy also towards international issues not immediately concerning them. The United Kingdom and other candidate countries have joined in this exchange of political views. The Foreign Ministers have decided to continue their efforts to coordinate foreign policy and to hold conferences periodically. In the meantime, in detailed discussions, the Committee formed by the Directors of the Foreign Ministries' Political Departments has further developed the consultation mechanism. This is a first step along the road towards a new style of diplomacy which directly short circuits the Foreign Ministries in an almost revolutionary manner.

(b) The negotiations on entry with the United Kingdom are now in their decisive phase. There was a high degree of unanimity in the talks Chancellor Brandt and I had with Prime Minister Heath on April 5, 1971, in Bonn. Both the six EEC partners and the United Kingdom hope for an early decision on Britain's accession to the European Communities.

If the difficult material problems are solved, the United Kingdom could become a member of the European Communities on January 1, 1973, and thereafter participate fully in all decisions on the further development. The difficult material problems include, in particular, that of the United Kingdom's financial participation during the period of transition.

In spite of all—to a certain extent considerable—difficulties, a positive decision will in the long run be of advantage to all if the enlargement and further development are not at the expense of the Community's institutional cohesion. A dynamically larger market including the British technological potential and international industrial experience will strengthen Europe's position in the world. With its tremendous industrial production, a uniform Western European market will be an inestimable stabilizing factor in the world. However, for its own well-understood interests, the enlarged Community must also realize to a special degree that it is a community open to the world, counteracting a possible trend towards greater obstacles to international trade.

(c) On February 9, 1971, in Brussels we were able to agree on the establishment of a European economic and monetary union, thus taking a vital step towards the completion of the work of European integration. By 1980 a domestic market embracing all members of the EEC, with free traffic in goods, labour and capital and with a uniform economic policy and a uniform currency will be in being. The necessary economic and monetary policy functions will be transferred to organs of the Communities and be controlled by the European Parliament. This in the long run will be an agent stimulating the political union of Europe.

From the very beginning, the logical further development of Europe towards structures superseding the nation-State was the basis of the policy of the present Federal Government. After all that has taken place in Western Europe since 1970, this should be obvious to everybody. An end has been put to the conflict of Germany's foreign policy, which until after the First World War fluctuated between opting for the West or the East. This is demonstrated by the history of the Federal Republic's foreign relations. Nor have any objective preconditions for such an option existed at all since the end of the Second World War or within the scope of the balance, then making its appearance, between deterrence and the ideological antagonism. However, the well-known British publicist Kenneth Younger has raised the question whether the Federal Republic is not drawing away from Western Europe, and this, above all, at a time when the United Kingdom is drawing nearer towards it. The development shows that there is no justification for this anxiety. For this, no one has the political will; nor would it be sensible in the present constellation. Only our link with Western Europe and its progressive strengthening make any active policy at all towards Eastern Europe possible.

The Soviet Union must note this. I have spent many hours talking about this with Mr. Gromyko, most recently during his visit to Kronberg, outside Frankfurt, last October. I have left him in no doubt that the progressive integration of Western Europe is a reality.

On the other hand, our *Ostpolitik* has also helped to make firmer links in the European Community possible. Not until our European partners were sure that they could not be drawn into our controversy with Eastern Europe were they prepared to associate their fate still more irrevocably with ours.

2. The Defence Alliance and the relationship with the United States constitute the other bases of our foreign policy. On these alone is our security founded. Only on these bases can the Federal Republic pursue foreign policy. By herself she cannot establish the necessary stability for herself; nor can she contribute towards détente on a non-alliance basis. Were she not a member of an alliance she would become a puppet of stronger Powers. The Soviet Union is also aware of this. We have made it quite clear that, just as the further development of the integration of Western Europe, so does our membership in the Defence Alliance and its build-up form a basis for the transaction of our treaties with her and the other States of Eastern Europe.

To a gratifying degree, even if not by chance, co-operation within NATO has, particularly in 1970, become stabilized.

In the Alliance, a medium-term perspective of growing European participation is beginning to develop. The starting-point for this was President Nixon's message containing the promise to continue to station American troops in Europe. Without America's military presence there is no balance, no security, in Europe; nor, therefore, any détente.

On December 2, 1970, decisions were taken about NATO's infrastructure programme (EDIP). When I visited London, on February 4 and 5, 1971, we managed to secure agreement with Britain on the foreign exchange offset. We agreed to solve this troublesome question, constantly recurring at short intervals, for a longer period—five years. This, in its turn, made the way clear for British participation in the NATO infrastructure programme. I am convinced that in the relationship with the United States it will also be possible to arrive at an agreement on the offsetting of foreign exchange. The two partners to the Alliance should jointly endeavour to settle once and for all the "evergreen" of the call for the unilateral withdrawal of American troops.

We Germans are willing to work for common security in the Alliance. The cohesion of NATO cannot be maintained without the defence efforts of all. At the same time, we wish to help towards developing a common conception of the Alliance for the policy of détente. In recent years, NATO has been transformed in a gratifying manner from a Defence Alliance to a Military Policy Alliance within the framework of which not only are defence matters settled but a common, forward-looking policy of détente is also developed. A straight line leads from the Reykjavik conference via that in Rome to that in Brussels. First reactions to the Warsaw Pact show that this development in NATO towards an alliance taking present circumstances into account and persisting even in the age of negotiations is also appreciated by the Warsaw Pact States.

We consider it particularly important that the partners to the Alliance should come to an agreement on the themes "Conference on European Security" and "Mutual Balanced Forces Reductions" (MBFR). For this it is necessary to develop a credible Western initiative. Such a common initiative should counteract onesided alterations in balance.

Relations among the partners to the Alliance, particularly those with the United States, must be steadily fostered. It would be a mistake to think they are so much a matter of course that it is not necessary to cultivate them further. Let us take, for instance, the complex problem of the relations between the European Communities and the United States. Here it is partly a question of psychological or atmospheric problems and partly of concrete questions of a balancing of economic interests. With all the criticism of the European Communities that has recently made its appearance in the United States, it should not be overlooked that the Common Market has greatly stimulated all the United States' exports. The European Communities are the United States' most important trading partner.

However, to clear up individual problems we must intensify the dialogue through more reciprocal information and consultation. I myself have been making efforts along these lines in various bodies of the European Communities. However, not every question can be settled to the satisfaction of all. For example, however much in need of development the common agricultural policy may be, it is one of the most important staples of the European Communities and, therefore, of the European integration policy. Additional problems will be posed in this area through the accession of the United Kingdom to the European Communities. What is at stake here, as in the EEC's association policy, is to trend towards an EEC that is open to the world and to prevent the revival of a destructively operating protectionism on the part of the Americans. With consideration given to domestic policy, fiscal policy and, particularly, foreign policy aspects, we must jointly find a middle way.

3. The third element in our foreign policy is our policy of détente towards Eastern Europe. This is planned to cover a long period. Because in this area a certain need to make up leeway existed, it took on, for many political commentators, a spectacular character in the first months of the formation of the present Govern-

ment in Bonn. In point of fact it can result only in success if it is pursued unwaveringly in dogged, minute detail.

It is necessary to pass through the following stages: Removal of existing disadvantages; balancing of interests wherever possible; increasing understanding; co-operation in specific areas. We are only at the start of this journey. Nevertheless, the international response to our efforts shows that we are understood. Only recently I found this confirmed in talks with five Foreign Ministers from Latin America.

The acid test of the process of détente is Berlin. At the Ambassadors' meeting on February 8, 1971, a concrete and comprehensive proposal was submitted by our Three Western Allies. On March 28, 1971, the Soviet Union, for her part, put forward a Paper for discussion. The Western position continues to include the securing of unimpeded access, the improvement of intra-city communications, the safeguarding of the existing links between the Federation and Berlin, and the arrangements for the representation of Berlin abroad.

In recent times there has been a certain propagandistic attack on the Berlin negotiations in general and the connection between a satisfactory settlement of this question and the ratification of the Moscow and Warsaw Treaties in particular. It is idle to waste time on delving into what constitutes the reasons for these pronouncements and statements on this side or the other. What, in our view, is material is that there has been no change in the Soviet attitude towards continuing the policy of détente in Europe. This has been demonstrated by the course taken at the Soviet Union's Communist Party Conference. Brezhnev and Gromyko made it clear that the Soviet Union attaches a crucial significance to the European peace order and international détente. The Soviet policy is planned on a long-term basis. Tactical movements do not come unexpected. They are precisely a signal that the Berlin negotiations

have reached a concrete stage. Neither the Federal Republic nor her Western Allies are being subjected to pressure. It is not a question of being able to refer at short notice to any result of negotiation but simply and solely of the permanent assurance of Berlin's viability. To achieve this we shall struggle along with patience, flexibility and perseverance. For people who allow themselves to be made nervous by a war of nerves, the words of President Truman apply: "Anyone who can't stand heat does not belong in the kitchen".

What is to be placed on record is that our policy of détente vis-à-vis Eastern Europe can already display certain results. It has raised our standing in Eastern Europe, and in the Third World countries as well. With the conclusion of the Treaty, the Polish Government has shown an understanding of our wishes for family reunion and the resettlement of persons of German origin. In the relationship with the Soviet Union the contacts of German scientists and the trips made by scientific and technical experts have increased. Negotiations on air travel and commercial agreements and consular arrangements are being conducted with the Soviet Union. We are also having talks with Czechoslovakia.

Our prospects for trade with Eastern Europe have improved; no dramatic increase is to be expected. The financing of large projects is causing our partners difficulties, although we cannot, and will not, make budgetary funds available for the financing of commercial projects. Nevertheless, a slow, steady increase in our trade with the Soviet Union and Eastern Europe is possible. For the Soviet Union, which in economic matters allows herself to be guided by a marked planning scheme, the Moscow Treaty is the basis for a steady development of commercial relations. We know that Moscow has not forgotten the case about an embargo on pipes in 1962, when the business, planned to cover a long period, was brusquely cancelled. The Soviet Union would also like to initiate a technological exchange within the framework of political information.

III. The position of the Federal Republic, her foreign policy, is the product of a large number of constants and variables. I have mentioned the most important constants: the further development of the process of integration in Western Europe, our responsibility within the Atlantic Alliance, and our participation in preserving peace in Europe. Because of our situation, and on the strength of our historical past, factors of interdependence in our foreign policy are necessarily more pronounced than is autonomy.

No foreign policy is static and divorced from one's own social and institutional development. In the case of the Federal Republic too it is important to cast a glance at the situation of our society and our system of government in order to understand our foreign policy.

A retrospective glance at the 1960s shows that, over a lengthy period, at least since the end of the 1950s, the contemplation of the citizens of the Federal Republic of foreign policy was determined by contradiction. In the official diction, the fictitious political standard was maintained that the restoration of the unity of our country was possible by free association, with the retention of the claim to the frontiers as they existed in 1937. For this policy, the support of our Allies was to be maintained. However, at the same time the normal political behaviour did not match up to this standard. Claims which were not justified in politics were preserved. The Federal Government to which I belong has taken the steps to resolve this contradiction. We have done so in the awareness that the German nation in its democratic forms is sufficiently strong to accept reality.

Doubts were entertained as to whether these steps were possible. Even in 1970 the French expert on Germany, M. Grosser, raised the question in the American journal "Foreign Affairs": "The German political system is more fragile than the French: the French State cannot be threatened by a conflict over its definition as nation, whereas the democracy in the Federal Republic is not secured against a crisis arising out of the German problem". The development since the forming of the present Federal Government indicates that the German democracy does have the stability expected by us. There has been no extremism among the expellee associations over the Treaty with Warsaw and the statement that the Oder-Neisse Line constitutes Poland's western frontier. The extreme right-wing party is nearing its end. Although militant left-wing and right-wing extremists have put in an appearance on the fringes, as they also do in other countries, they do not constitute a danger for our democracy. The prospects of the Federal Republic establishing for herself an appropriate role in the international setting and acting in a constructive manner are not poor.

Lecture given by the Federal Minister of Food, Agriculture and Forestry, Josef Ertl, at the Annual Meeting of the Germany/Switzerland Chamber of Commerce in Zurich on June 18, 1971, on the Theme "The Common Market and European Integration" (Excerpt)

I. The fathers of the Treaties of Rome had one objective that remains unchanged: to develop and enlarge the European Economic Community until political union was achieved. The foundation stone was laid with the integration of one part of the economy—namely, agriculture. Economic and monetary union were to follow.

If today we draw up a balance sheet, on the credit side we record:

- The Agricultural Community—the Common Agricultural Market—is established.
- Since the conference at The Hague at the end of 1969 the Community has been making great efforts to establish an economic and monetary union in the course of a phased plan.
- The negotiations on the enlargement of the Community by the accession of the United Kingdom, Ireland, Denmark and Norway are under way. The recent talks between the French President Pompidou and the British Prime Minister Heath allow for the expectation that it will be possible shortly to settle the final questions still open concerning the entry of the United Kingdom.
- As the form to be taken by the political union of the Ten, the federation is emerging in outline.

On the debit side of the balance sheet, the following shortages or obstacles are still recorded:

- The still isolated construction of the Agricultural Market.
- The situation regarding the varying interests of the Member States so far as the importance of agricultural prices are concerned for domestic policy.
- The lack of a common aim in relation to market prospects of the Member States because of varying assessments of stability and inflation.
- The resultant peculiar susceptibility of agricultural prices tied to the green dollar to the effects of a change in currency parity rates.
- In the institutional sphere, the frequent antagonisms between the Council of Ministers and the Commission and the lack of a genuine parliamentary control.

The integration of the Community is, therefore, by no means concluded. Doubtless this process can, and will, still take decades before the goal is reached. Nevertheless, in the 14 years since the conclusion of the treaty on the establishment of the European Economic Community, significant progress has been made. The clasp holding Europe together, the Common Agricultural Market, has remained, and still remains, intact despite the devaluation of the franc and the upward revaluation of the DM in 1969 and despite the floating of exchange rates recently necessary in the Federal Republic and the Netherlands.

Customs duties, levies with the same effect, and restrictions on quantities have been basically abolished in the commercial transactions among the Community's Member States, thereby laying the foundations for free trade in an economic area of a size Europe has never yet known in its long history. The Community's great economic and attractive power is the result of this integration.

The full integration of the agricultural markets and the Community's financial solidarity in the sphere of agriculture form the political prerequisites for free trade inside the Community. Both have been achieved; and doubtless I do not exaggerate if I say that this was the most difficult chapter so far in the coalescing of the Member States to form a single community.

I am convinced that what has so far been achieved can endure only if further progress in integration is made. From this results a compulsion to urge the Community's continued development and strength further forward. Initial important steps in this direction have already been taken. They allow me to hope that the Community can overcome the critical stage of an integration that is too weak and onesided and relying, in particular, on the agricultural policy. In this connection I am thinking primarily of the phased plan for the establishment of an economic and monetary union, which was approved last February after a hard struggle.

Even in the course of this present decade a uniform economic and monetary area in which passenger, goods, services and capital traffic can operate without competitive distortions is to be established. The necessary decisions on economic policy will be taken at Community level. The Community organs will be furnished with the necessary powers. These are tremendous tasks with which we are now faced. After all, it is a matter of overcoming, in a relatively short time, differences, and even antagonisms, which have developed over the centuries and of urging on the union of Europe in the economic and political spheres. The appreciation of this is the precondition for not being discouraged by occasional temporary difficulties and stagnations and also for taking proper account of the prevailing circumstances, whether they be economic or political.

In the middle of this process of the internal stabilization and progressive integration of the Community come the negotiations on its enlargement. In these negotiations it must be ensured that the indispensable dynamic development of the Community is promoted through the accession of additional countries. I believe that it is possible to attain this objective. All States prepared to accede have declared their readiness to abide by the Treaties of Rome, including the consequential legislation. The negotiations are now concentrated on laying down the conditions for the period of adjustment to Community law. To this extent it has also been possible to make good progress. Remaining for solution are, in particular, problems concerning financing and the importation of dairy produce from New Zealand.

In the event of the enlargement of the Community, appropriate solutions must be found for the countries which are closely associated with the countries acceding and which would be faced by difficulties unless special arrangements were made. In this connection, the countries in question include the Commonwealth countries and the EFTA countries not acceding—

and thus Switzerland as well. I shall later on go again into the aspects which could be decisive for an agreement between Switzerland and the EEC in the agricultural sector. As a Community of six States, the EEC already has a great commercial policy responsibility. One subject of criticism, particularly on the part of the United States, is the EEC's preference, agricultural and association policy. It will be a matter of eliminating misunderstandings in the course of a constant dialogue and of achieving the necessary balancing of opposing interests.

III. About two months ago, the Council of Ministers in Brussels agreed on a basic decision to introduce common measures in the sphere of agricultural structural and social policy, thus supplementing the common marketing and price policy. The agreement came after years of considerable wrangling.

At first, the Community's countries with a high industrial development, in which many of the measures now agreed are already being implemented on a national basis, for the reasons given above adopted a very restrained attitude towards the structural and social measures. My own country was one of these. For this attitude three fears were responsible:

- in the first place, there was the danger that, as a result of the harmonization of the measures at Community level, the necessary national scope for taking the different regional circumstances into account would be lost;

- secondly, indeterminable financial burdens for the Community would result;

- thirdly, an immediate and simultaneous implementation of all measures entailing a large financial participation on the part of the Community would be at variance with the gradual development of the Community into an economic and monetary union. In the event of a further isolated integration of agriculture, the tensions and distortions

I have described, which have already resulted for agriculture because of the inadequate integration in the non-agricultural spheres, would become intensified.

It was possible to take these fears into account through constructive co-operation when the Council was taking basic decisions. It was, in particular, ensured that the necessary national scope should be preserved—above all, for regional measures—and that the measures should be implemented only within the scope of a limited and determinable financial expenditure. It can be said that, with this, my ideas largely prevailed.

I have described these various aspects of the agricultural structural and social policy so fully because they are of such fundamental importance for the common agricultural policy. I hope that, on the strength of the decisions on prices and structure that were taken in March, it will be possible the more easily to solve also the problem of the national subventions which have recently caused us much anxiety. All Member States have instituted in their own countries an almost unsurveyable number of measures for benefiting agriculture. Insofar as they distort competition in the Community it is urgently necessary to abolish them. A harmonization of the investment aids is also required; otherwise the Common Agricultural Market will tend to fall into national hands and thus be seriously jeopardized. Here the Commission of the European Communities is faced by a big task.

The problem of surpluses, which in recent years has made the headlines time and again, has latterly retired more into the background. The Community has succeeded in reducing the surplus stocks, although it must be admitted that this was possible only with the help of considerable financial expenditure. Nevertheless, the disposal of the stocks must not conceal the fact that we shall have to continue to reckon with a surplus production in the case of soft wheat, barley, milk, sugar and certain kinds of fruit.

The main cause of the production of surpluses is that it was possible to increase agricultural output enormously on the strength of technical and scientific progress, but, unlike the position in the case of industrial commodities, it is impossible correspondingly to increase the demand for foodstuffs. A solution of the problem of surpluses with the assistance of drastic price reductions is out of the question. On the contrary, in view of the social situation of agriculture, we have been compelled to raise prices. Unless one has recourse to the extremely problematic fixing of production quotas, the problem of surpluses can, in my opinion, be solved only by a reorientation of production towards products in short supply and, above all, with the assistance of structural and social measures leading to a better structure of agriculture. Modernized farms are more able to adapt their products to demand, although it is possible that the higher productivity of modernized farms, and the compulsion to produce, will in their turn lead again to surpluses. Here, however, we have to do with a very long process. It is hardly possible today to gauge the effect of an enlargement of the Community on the problem of surpluses. Much will depend on the still-awaited result of the negotiations on the importation of dairy produce from New Zealand and of sugar from the Commonwealth sugar-producing countries and, on the other hand, on how the producers and consumers in the countries acceding will react to higher agricultural prices.

Closely connected with the problem of surpluses is the problem of financing the common agricultural policy, which costs a great deal of money. At present, the agricultural budget, which this year amounts to about 2,700 million units of account, makes up about 90% of the Community's total budget. This shows how onesided has been this Community's development so far. We hope that we shall soon arrive at savings in the matter of assisting the agricultural market. In the long run, however, the Community's expenditure in implementing the agricultural and social policy will increase, although the Council has decided to make do, at least in the first years, with the funds already earmarked for this policy.

IV. After having described the internal problems posed by the integration of the Community in such detail, it will be easier to understand the problems posed quite generally with regard to the Community's agricultural trade with Third Countries.

I think that a Community is legitimately concerned to encourage the sale of its own products rather than to import products. Other countries, Switzerland for example, also avail themselves of this right within their national sphere. Of course, in the case of surplus products this preference of the Community for the sale of its own products leads to corresponding difficulties in the case of the importation of these products from Third Countries. The attacks of the Third Countries affected are, therefore, directed less against the policy of preference than against the mere agricultural policy of the Community. Therefore, the Community's policy of preference is attacked when it increasingly concludes agreements on association with a large number of Third Countries for which political reasons are often the determining factor. I have just described how difficult it is to solve the problem of surpluses and how it can be solved only on a long-term basis. These problems are a consequence of the traditional agricultural structure in Europe. Switzerland also is familiar with these problems. It cannot be expected that the problems can be solved overnight.

I also believe that many attacks directed against us by Third Countries—particularly the United States—are onesided, and certainly over-emphasized. For example, one subject of criticism is that every year the Community has an excess production of about five million tons of soft wheat. However, this criticism is due to falsely relating the prices of grain in the Community to the amount to be borne by the price of fodder. Altogether, in the case of grain, the Community needs something like seven million tons more. Although in recent years grain imports have declined, this circumstance must be placed against the fact that the imports of vegetable fats, which are substitute products for fodder grain, have greatly increased. In recent years the United States alone has been able to more than double her exports of soya to the EEC. Altogether in recent years the Community's agricultural imports have increased, even if not, by far, as much as the imports of industrial commodities. The reason is, in particular, the elasticity that is lacking in the demand for foodstuffs.

I think that, in general, there is no justification for speaking of an agricultural protectionism within the EEC.

In conclusion, I would like to say a word about various aspects which might be determinant for an arrangement between Switzerland and the EEC in the agricultural sector. I have already pointed out that the question of a trading arrangement with Switzerland is posed, above all, in connection with the negotiations on the enlargement of the EEC. In Brussels, exploratory talks were carried out with the EFTA countries which have not applied for entry to the EEC, in order to gain a clear picture of the possibilities of coming to an agreement with these States.

The talks with Switzerland have established that there is still no question of her adopting the EEC agricultural policy. In the Federal Republic of Germany we appreciate that, with the present agricultural level and the present conditions governing costs and structure, Switzerland takes the standpoint that she does not and cannot agree to a reduction of the net income of her farmers by about one half . . . .

V. The Federal Republic of Germany, with political factors very much in mind, has energetically advocated the initiation of negotiations on the enlargement of the Community. She is prepared to find acceptable conditions in the course of the negotiations. The very amicable talks Prime Minister Heath recently had with Federal Chancellor Brandt in Bonn must be regarded in the light of this attitude of my country. I can assure you that, with regard to their special political situation, this is the attitude the Federal Republic of Germany also adopts in the case of those EFTA countries which do not seek accession to the Community.

We must all help to achieve the greatest possible union in Europe at all levels. Europe cannot in the long run consist of a community of six or of ten.

Without euphoria, with a realistic assessment of the facts, but with a will to succeed, we should all move, step by step, towards the great community guaranteeing prosperity and security which is what we consider Europe still to be.

Lecture given by the Federal Chancellor on June 25, 1971, in Bonn at the Meeting of the Members of the German Society for Foreign Policy on the Theme "Topical Questions of German Foreign Policy" (Excerpt)

Enlargement and Internal Development of the European Community

On Wednesday morning (June 23, 1971), in Luxembourg, agreement was reached about all the essential modalities concerning the participation of the United Kingdom in the operations of the Community, and thereby of her entry. This is a step of great importance. The enlargement, about which there has been controversy and wrestling for years, is now taking on concrete forms.

None of us will underestimate the hurdles the British Government still has to take in domestic politics, but my assessment is that Britain's entry will not break down on the British themselves. At any rate I wish those who support the entry the success that is needed in the interest of the common cause.

It will be clear to anyone who looks back on January, 1963, or on December, 1967, that here is a memorable breakthrough. This also paves the way for the other three applicants—Denmark, Norway and Ireland—into the Community. The Europe of the Six will become a Europe of the Ten. This has a significance both economic and political.

Allow me to take this opportunity to refer to the constructive role played by the French Government in the efforts to resolve the questions connected with Britain's entry. We have had many a high word amicably about them. Now the die is cast. I would like to congratulate all who have contributed towards the result that has been achieved in common and made possible, not least by the British Government's clear looking towards Europe.

Now that the entry of the United Kingdom and the others is within reach, many are cogitating on the fact that the enlargement of the Community will entail not only advantages but also fresh problems. Certainly it is not easier to reconcile the views of ten States than it is to achieve a consensus among six. It must not, however, be overlooked that the advantages far outweigh the disadvantages. The enlargement will increase the strength of the Community, promote social progress, strengthen its democratic foundation, and increase its weight in international politics.

Here and there it has been possible to read

that Britain's entry is necessary and has become possible in order to prevent a German hegemony in the Community. This is nonsense. The realities in Western Europe tolerate no reversion to the ideas prevailing in the last century. They call for partnership on equal terms.

The dynamism the Community has taken on again, after a period of standing still, is also shown in its ability tenaciously to urge its internal development forward. After the completion of the customs union by the date envisaged, the Community has now embarked on the road towards economic and monetary union, which, in its integral parts, is to become a reality even in this present decade.

As decided by the Council of Ministers, the harmonization of economic policy has now been approved. In the case of the contemplated harmonization of monetary policy, there has, for well-known reasons, been some delay. I would like, however, to make it clear that the temporary floating of the exchange rates does not militate against the common objective. We have to keep our own house in order; but, with our measures, we remain within the framework of the Community and are earnestly endeavouring to evolve a common European policy, precisely in this important area as well.

Notable progress has been achieved in recent months in the area of political co-operation. Last November the Member States—and with the prospect of the enlargement—started coordinating their foreign policy in important areas. We ourselves and the other Governments have still to adapt ourselves fully to this new procedure. This holds good for the members of the Community internally; it also holds good externally for the Community if it wishes to exert its opinions uniformly and thereby take appropriate account of the interests of others.

Our concept, to create a Europe of realities, has stood the test and resulted in successes. Since the conference at The Hague we have been able to help to set in motion a development which was not overcharged with ideology but which led to practical results. We have always remained furnished with initiatives; the step-by-step process has proved to be the right one. Not for one moment have we left out of sight the goal of a European Government that is competent to perform legal acts in the areas of common policy and whose official actions are parliamentarily controlled.

I am glad that in a few days' time I shall have an opportunity to discuss the position, the next steps and the perspectives of the European union with President Pompidou and Prime Minister Chaban-Delmas.

The United States and Europe

In the meantime, new tasks have presented themselves. During my talks in the United States last week, it became clear that the development in Western Europe finds much interest there, even if it is also causing anxieties. This does not apply, or scarcely applies, to the Government, even if otherwise one frequently meets with the question as to whether the Community could not cut itself off to the disadvantage of those outside.

Well, it can easily be proved that the economic relations of the United States with the existing Community have developed favourably. Everything speaks for the fact that these will not, in any event, deteriorate through the enlargement of the Community. An open commercial policy lies in Europe's interest.

Precisely in the relationship with the United States must unnecessary conflicts of interests be avoided, and, where this is not possible, the divergencies must be mitigated and reduced to their natural proportions. What is gained by European co-operation must not be at the expense of the Atlantic partnership.

It must be made known objectively that arrangements must be concerted with those EFTA countries which will not be becoming members of the European Community. This has nothing to do with discrimination; we cannot allow new trading barriers to make their appearance. Certain aspects resulting from associations in other parts of the world are complicated.

Independently of this, no one will be able to ignore the fact that the growing Europe must also assume a growing responsibility in international politics. For the United States this, in the long run, is also the most important starting-point for arriving at any relief.

President Nixon is still greatly interested in a strengthening of the European components in the Alliance. The programme for improving security in Europe, initiated a few months ago, is praised for its significance in principle. In the wish for a balancing of efforts within the Alliance, the interests of the Americans coincide with the interests of the majority of European partners. Nevertheless, as the leading Protection Power, our American allies cannot be replaced. The presence of American troops also remains indispensable for common security in the Alliance . . .

One final remark: I mean—to know what is, and what is not, possible. We must always find the right proportion, something which in our history we have all too often found hard. A Federal Republic of Germany which is self-reliant, strengthened, internally consolidated, secure in the protection of the Alliance, embedded and responsibly assisting in shaping a prospering European Community—this will be a powerful factor for ensuring peace in Europe.

Statement of the Federal Chancellor before the German Bundestag on June 24, 1971

Mr. President, Ladies and Gentlemen,

In my Government Policy Statement of October 28, 1969, I said, with reference to the then impending summit conference at The Hague:

The peoples of Europe are waiting for and urging the statesmen to supplement the logic of history by the determination for success.

This has taken place in an important area. Early yesterday, in the final round of discussions in Luxembourg, the six Member States of the Community and the United Kingdom reached agreement on the enlargement. This means that an important victory has been won for the European ideal. All the Governments concerned and the Commission have made their constructive contribution towards this victory.

As already after the conference at The Hague, allow me before this House to give particular prominence to the statesmanlike far-sightedness of the French President Georges Pompidou, but for whose crucial contribution this success would not have been possible.

The same is to be said of Prime Minister Heath. His Government has abided by the decision of its predecessor and has followed it tenaciously. It has demonstrated that the United Kingdom wishes to enter the Community without any reservations concerning the Community's aims and options. With this, it was possible to clear crucial difficulties out of the way.

In the final analysis, the success is to be sought in the clear political will of all the politicians concerned to continue together the association in the manner initiated by the European

Community, which, despite all, has led to such a great success.

So far as we ourselves are concerned, I would like in this hour to express the thanks of the Federal Government to Federal Minister Walter Scheel and his staff for the perseverance, the negotiating skill and the wealth of ideas with which they have contributed towards this success.

The success of the negotiations on enlargement is also evidence of the strength of the Community. Now, it will grow beyond the geographic limitations which were conditioned at the time of its foundation by the political circumstances. Had the Community not produced this strength, there would have been strong—and justified—criticism. Conversely, the outcome of the negotiations demonstrates that the revolutionary proposal put forward in May, 1950, by Robert Schuman, together with Jean Monnet, is a first and strategically important step.

If, in this hour—which can without exaggeration be called historic—I mention with gratitude these two names, allow me also to recall those of the then Federal Chancellor Adenauer and the Italian Prime Minister de Gasperi, who so persistently helped to initiate union in Western Europe.

Here a member of this House should also be mentioned for his pioneering activity in the European Community. I mean Professor Walter Hallstein, the first—and for many years—President of the Commission.

In December, 1969, I made it clear at The Hague that it was our view that the future of the Community also depended—and precisely—on whether it would succeed in its enlargement. At the same time, in the months since then we have all left no doubt that the entry could be sought and realized only if the solidarity between the six members of the Community were fully preserved. In the course of the certainly not always easy negotiations, we succeeded in various kinds of contacts—personal as well—to discuss with our partners ways and means which could benefit the actual negotiations on entry.

What has been achieved in these days will also have a favourable effect on the further development of the Community towards an economic and monetary union.

The Federal Government will do everything in its power to bring to a conclusion satisfactory to all concerned the forthcoming negotiations on the entry of Denmark, Norway and Ireland by the end of the year.

At the same time we shall make every effort to see that the special relationship with those EFTA members which are not seeking entry is settled by the time the negotiations on entry are concluded, so that these important treaties can also become operative with the accession of the Four.

The Federal Government is convinced that the enlarged and—as we are satisfied—internally consolidating Community must be open to the world in the economic sphere and that it must show that it is able to measure up to its responsibility in world politics.

Without any doubt, an enlarged and strengthened Community has an influence on the world political scene. Perhaps many an observer outside has realized more clearly than we—and others in Western Europe—the importance this Community can have in world events.

The European Community will pursue a policy of peace. How could it be otherwise for the European peoples, in view of their historical experiences?

In the days to come it will be a task of the European Community not to neglect the Atlantic Alliance and the partnership with the United States, but also to prove itself, wherever this is possible, a reliable partner for the Eastern European countries.

I believe that all in Germany should have occasion in feeling satisfaction at this momentous step forward.

Statement of the Federal Minister for Foreign Affairs, Walter Scheel, on June 23, 1971, in Luxembourg, on the Results of the Negotiations on Accession

In the early hours of this morning it was possible to conclude an important round in the negotiations on accession with the United Kingdom. Those concerned can be satisfied. It was possible to achieve a good and fair compromise in meeting the interests both of the Community and of the countries prepared to accede.

This means that already this year Europe has taken the second crucial step towards union. After the decisions taken on February 9, 1971, on the establishment of the economic and monetary union, this June 23 signifies that the United Kingdom can now enter the Common Market. The negotiations on this started close on a year ago.

With this, the period lying behind us is the most successful since the foundation of the EEC. The time schedule drawn up at the conference at The Hague in December, 1969, has not proved too ambitious. We have even achieved more than many expected. The development has proved that those whose confidence in the strength of the European ideal remained unbroken were right.

We have been accused of being too optimistic. This often happens when the endeavour

is to achieve concrete aims for ideals. However, far-distant goals can also be reached with energy and tenacity. In intensive minute work, in hard struggling for individual solutions, the "concrete Utopia" in a united Europe is being realized.

All concerned, the Member Governments, the British Government and, in particular, the Commission of the European Communities, have contributed towards the common success. All were determined not this time to fail again. Even if in essence the negotiations were hard, they were conducted in a communal spirit.

German diplomacy can also find satisfaction on this day. Its constant endeavour to eliminate obstacles on principle and to arrive at a practical compromise has borne fruit.

The enlargement of the EEC can be the decisive political event of this century in Europe. With it, not only a European market of the size and importance of the American comes into being. It is also the foundation on which Europe is able to bring an influence to bear in the world as a factor of stability and peace.

Today we have taken a step that can have historic significance.

Statement of the Federal Minister of Economics and Finance, Prof. Dr. Karl Schiller, on June 23, 1971, on the Result of the Negotiations on the Accession of the United Kingdom to the European Community

With the successful outcome of the Luxembourg conference on the accession of the United Kingdom to the Community of the Six, Europe has taken an important step nearer to the goal of its self-realization. The solution of the central political problems of Britain's entry must be regarded as the key to the positive conclusion

not only of the negotiations with the United Kingdom but also of those with Denmark, Norway and Ireland. It is also the prerequisite for a close economic association of the enlarged Community with those States of the European Free Trade Association—EFTA—which, for special reasons, have not applied for membership in the Community—in particular the neutral countries Switzerland, Sweden and Austria.

Not yet have all questions been clarified, and in the end the Parliaments will have the last word. It can now, however, be said with satisfaction that, following the decisions on the internal development of the Community—namely, the gradual realization of the economic and monetary union—only a few months later has a crucial breakthrough to the enlargement of the Community been achieved. More than ever can we be confident that the anachronistic rift between EEC and EFTA is finally overcome and Europe is growing into an economic dimension that, besides the political, is of decisive significance for its future between the Great Powers.

Interview of the Federal Chancellor with the French Newspaper "Le Monde" of July 6, 1971 (Excerpt)

Question:

Mr. Chancellor, do you think that the entry of the United Kingdom and the other countries prepared to accede to the European Community that has now become probable will result in the centuries-old differences between the three large nations of Western Europe being finally settled and the détente with the East facilitated? How do you visualize the development of Europe's relations with the United States?

Answer:

The enlargement of the European Community by the United Kingdom and the other three countries opens a new chapter in the history of Europe and sets the seal on the fact that the national and nation-State rivalries in Western Europe now belong to the past and that there is a serious desire for economic and political union.

I am not one of those who thought that the improvement in the relations between Paris and London must be at the expense of the relations of London with Bonn or of Paris with Bonn.

I am convinced that not only do we need the trustful co-operation of the three European countries with the greatest economic strength but that all European partners will, and will have to, play their own, and equally important, roles in this co-operation that is now becoming closer.

In my opinion the establishment of more cordial relations between the Eastern and the Western half of our continent can only in the end favourably influence the perspectives of the enlargement and the strengthening of union in Western Europe. It is no secret that the Soviet Union is suspicious of, above all, the political implications of our alliance. However, speaking objectively, it is a fact that the effects of this alliance are conducive to the preservation of peace.

So far as the United States is concerned, I have recently pointed out in Washington and New York that, despite the great changes that have taken place in Europe and the world, the basic elements in the relationship between Western Europe and the United States have remained unchanged. Both partners need one another today just as twenty years ago, and both also need the balance of forces in the relationship with the East. The partial difficulties resulting here and there from the development of the European Community should not be exaggerated. The relations rest on the foundation of the consonance of the vital interests and convictions that have developed in the course of twenty years of co-operation. Nothing of this will change, even if—as we expect and hope—

Europe's political and economic weight grows. Europe will be able to bear a larger share of responsibility in international politics although it must never isolate itself.

Question:

Do you not fear that the conditions governing the enlargement of the European Community will result in certain principles on which the Community was established being jeopardized? For example, it seems that, according to statements made by Mr. Heath, France and the United Kingdom have come to an understanding to allow one point of the Rome Treaty which provides for majority decisions in important questions in the European Community's Council of Ministers to be conveniently "forgotten". Do you think it is right to set the seal on the rule of unanimity in this manner in the institutional practice of the European Community?

Answer:

The enlargement alters nothing of the legal situation in the Community, since the countries prepared to accede accept the Treaties in all their parts. The candidate countries have also expressly embraced the *"finalité politique"* of the work of integration. In the future European Community, when the competencies exceed those of the three original Communities, the set of instruments will be attuned to the experiences gained with the integration up to now.

Since the formulation of the Luxembourg Protocol, in which France on the one hand and the other members of the Community on the other expressed their attitude towards the employment of majority decisions, we have also achieved something decisive in the Community and adopted pioneering Resolutions in the Council of Ministers. We would have made no progress had we exhausted ourselves in a quarrel about procedural matters. Moreover, it seems to me to be a positive element that we are no longer squabbling about doctrinaire

questions but that we have decided on visualizing what can really be achieved in the coming years. If I am an advocate of a Europe of realities, it does not mean that I am losing sight of the political goal. This goal is the Political Community. And this includes—without any levelling of national identities—the creation of a rationally organized European Government which can take decisions in the spheres of common policy and is subject to parliamentary control.

Question:

President Pompidou hopes that an "intergovernmental" organization serves as the core of a confederated Europe. Do you agree with this hope, and, if so, which initiatives seem to you to meet this the best?

Answer:

The gradual establishment of the Political Union, of the future communal Western Europe, represents a process for which history displays no prototype. The classic difference between a confederation and a federal State is not likely to bring us much farther. Already the co-operation in the Community is something new in quality. In it, we have already elements of a European Government and forms of co-operation going beyond the classic intergovernmental co-operation.

Here I would merely like to refer to the direct application of the Ordinances of the Council and the Commission, to the European fiscal constitution, and to the phased plan for the establishment of the economic and monetary union. As is well-known, the phased plan provides in the final stage that Community organs can take radical decisions quickly and effectively and that this policy is subject to the control of the European Parliament.

It seems to me best if in this manner—i.e., on the basis of what has already been achieved—we strengthen the co-operation step by step and then also institutionalize it suitably. I believe that with this the goal we find ourselves in harmony with the ideas the French President has put forward in recent months.

Question:

Do you think that our generation will see the birth of a genuine European confederation? Do you think that this confederation will one day be concerned with the questions of defence? If you do, how do you visualize this extension and the role the Federal Republic could play in this connection?

Answer:

I believe our generation will see in an alliance, in the "Community" or whatever it may be called, binding decisions being taken for the spheres that can be pursued in common in a sensible form. The '70s will see great progress being made towards this goal.

Certainly one day a consolidated Europe will have to concern itself with defence tasks. It seems to me that the question as to how this is to happen is premature. Today, we must rather start with the role of the Western Europeans in the Atlantic Alliance. And we must naturally bear in mind the necessary partnership of Europe with the United States. It is inevitable and essential that the European members of the Alliance should assume more responsibility for the common security. A first beginning has already been made in this direction, and doubtless the efforts will have to be continued and intensified in the coming years.

In this connection, the Federal Republic of Germany will have no special role to play, but she will not shirk her responsibility. Moreover, I would also emphasize that the Federal Republic has renounced nuclear weapons.

Statement of the Federal Minister for Foreign Affairs, Walter Scheel, in the German Bundestag on July 19, 1971 (Excerpt)

. . . . .
I think we are all agreed that the year behind us has been one of the most successful in the development of the European Communities. If we compare what has been done and achieved last year with the commitments imposed on us by the Treaties and also with the aims we set ourselves at the conference at The Hague in December, 1969, we can be satisfied. The balance is good and full of perspectives for the future. Doubtless the most notable events of 1970 were the creation of a European fiscal constitution, with the Communities receiving their own revenues, the commencement to time of the negotiations on entry, the solution of the central problems concerning Britain's entry into the European Communities, and the decision to establish the Community's economic and monetary union.

No particular statements are needed in this House on the political significance of these decisions. Nor, I am happy to say, are there any differences of opinion on this score. It must, however, be stated that these results have been achieved only because the will to succeed and the political determination of all concerned proved stronger than such complicated economic or technical problems. The Community has demonstrated that it is able to accomplish great tasks, and this gives strength and confidence for further operations.

In this connection, I must expressly emphasize the outstanding spirit that has prevailed in the negotiations on the entry of the four future Member States of the Community. Here my special thanks are due to the French delegation, which presided in the first six months of 1971 and but for whose active help and readiness to mediate such gratifying and rapid progress could not have been made.

In connection with the meeting between President Pompidou and Prime Minister Heath, the Press has expressed anxiety whether the Anglo-French tête-à-tête could not initiate a new policy of the maintenance of equilibrium in the Community. The expression "entente cordiale" has been going the rounds. Well, if today there is indeed an entente cordiale, then it not the one from the beginning of the century but the entente cordiale that characterizes the whole of the EEC. It would be foolish to suspect that any serious statesman would today take it into his head to wish to pursue a balance of power policy in Europe.

I would like to wish the Italian presidency complete success in fulfilling the tasks assumed on July 1, and I assure it of our constant support for these tasks. The holding of the Chair in the Communities is not confined to the activity in Brussels, though that is responsible enough. It includes the task of making sure that the Community presents itself everywhere as an entity where diplomatic representations are active in the capitals of the world and at the headquarters of international organizations.

The second six months of this year have also posed the Community great tasks. Although much progress has been made in the negotiations on enlargement, much still remains open. We shall have to make great efforts if we wish to bring everything to a successful conclusion by the end of the year. We are following with deep concern and attention the discussion now flaring up in the countries that are prepared to accede. The intensity—indeed the passion—with which these interchanges are being conducted demonstrates afresh the tremendous political significance now inherent in the enlargement of the Community. In the opposing views, many arguments known to ourselves from our parliamentary debates on the establishment of the EEC are reappearing. It may, perhaps, be good for our colleagues in the countries pre-

pared to enter to know that many anxieties to which we gave expression in this House in 1957 have a different complexion for us now. The courageous step we then took with our partners has proved worth while. Not one of us would like to retrace our steps.

Therefore, we are hoping, confidently and trusfully, for a happy outcome of the discussions in the countries who wish to become members of the Community.

In the coming months an important part will be played by the negotiations on a settlement of the relations between the enlarged Community and the non-acceding EFTA countries. In the communiqué of The Hague we held out to these countries the prospect that it was our wish to seek close ties with them. Of course the Community's capacity to act must not be restricted by these ties. Between these two aims exists a certain strained relationship with which shall have to cope in future. The Community has now put forward proposals to the Member States on this complex and these we shall be discussing in the coming weeks, and for the first time in the Council sessions on July 26 and 27. We think that a free trade arrangement in the commercial sphere will best serve the interests of all concerned. An arrangement with this objective, which, beyond this, is to be capable of development and must conform to the GATT regulations, accords with the intention expressed by the Community in November, 1970, that no new fresh obstacles to trade should be erected. As the then President of the Council of the European Communities, I made a statement to this effect before the delegations of the States concerned.

The Federal Government will plead for a speedy treatment of these important questions so that the treaties with these countries can become operative simultaneously with the treaties of accession. However, in this connection it will also be necessary to bear in mind the interests of other countries whose trade is affected by the enlargement process. This particularly applies to our partners on the other side of the Atlantic, although indeed for all other countries which may possibly find themselves confronted by trading policy problems through the fresh developments in Europe.

During his visit to the United States, the Federal Chancellor once more assured the American President of our very great interest in improving co-operation between the United States and the Common Market. Many problems which are now being taken very seriously in the United States would appear far less serious if there were an improved level of information and if there were already an intensive contact between the Government of the United States and the Commission and other EEC bodies. We are, however, already on the road towards this.

In this connection, I think all members of the German Bundestag will welcome the fact that the Community, in the awareness of its responsibility—and precisely towards the developing countries—is the first of this world's trading powers to operate the general preferences for developing countries with effect from July 1 this year.

In view of the still unresolved monetary problems, with their eminent significance for the existence and the further development of the Community, we shall continue to concern ourselves about a Community solution, in the interests too of an agricultural market that is able to function. In this connection, I think we should not dramatize differences of opinion. After all, with the Brussels communiqué of May 9, the Community expressly allowed for the possibility of a limited floating of the exchange rate of the D-Mark.

The economic and monetary union is a ten-year project to be completed in stages. The main purpose of the initial stage, which has just commenced, is to enable the members to feel their way forward to the requirements of the subsequent stages. These requirements include unanimity about the objective of the policy of stability, since this Community wishes to be a stable Community, a Community of stability—and so it ought to be. If this unanimity is assured and successfully practised, unanimity in monetary policy no longer presents any problem. However, as long as that is not so, problems will continue to exist.

We are in agreement with our partners—particularly with France—that the Community should present itself to the world as quickly as possible as a self-reliant factor in terms of monetary policy. In every respect our proposals to ward off speculative inflows of capital by extending the band widths towards the outside have been of a communal nature. We have also supported them with concrete promises. We were, and are, ready to agree to an intervention system, harmonized on a Community basis, in the foreign exchange markets and possibly also to help to realize even earlier the European Fund for Co-operation in Monetary Policy, although, according to decisions so far taken, this is visualized only for a later date.

We are ready to go along with the administrative measures the Commission has proposed for warding off inflows of capital, although to be sure within the scope of our basic market economy attitude.

However, the present lack of unanimity in monetary policy has also had something good about it. We all now know better what is necessary for the economic and monetary union to be able to function. Let us hope, for later reflection, that it will remain an episode, a somewhat stony stretch on the road to the economic and monetary union . . .

The Community's co-operation in the sphere of foreign policy is taking place parallel to the integration in the European Communities and in an association, continually becoming closer, with the European Parliament and the European Commission. Since the approval of the Luxembourg Report on October 27, 1970, towards the realization of which the initiatives of the Federal Government made a considerable contribution, a mechanism of suitable consultations between the Six and an exchange of opinions between the Community States and the four candidate countries on important foreign policy issues has been set in motion as a first stage of political unity in Europe.

Apart from this, a number of practical measures resulting in a continually closer network of co-operation in foreign policy have been initiated. They will complement the actual consultation mechanism and guarantee its efficacy and continuity. Even if experiences to date are necessarily still limited, it can already be said that this form of co-operation in foreign policy will remain for a long time to come the way that promises that Europe will be able to speak with one voice.

Interview of the Federal Chancellor with the News Magazine "Der Spiegel" for the September 27, 1971, Edition (Excerpt)

Question:

Mr. Chancellor, what, according to your concept of foreign politics, will Europe look like in ten years' time?

Answer:

Even if I could, I must not awaken the impression that here is existing a Federal Republic whose Federal Chancellor says: Europe will look like this. The most I can say is that in this decade we shall do everything possible to overcome the confrontation in Western Europe so as at the same time to make progress with the integration of Western Europe.

We always regard this as an interdependent process. The chances are good that in this decade we can bring the enlarged EEC a vital step forward towards the economic and monetary union. And the chances are good that in this decade not only can a considerable amount of practical co-operation be realized between the States of Western and Eastern Europe but also that partial successes will be achieved in the balanced reduction of troops and armaments in Europe, especially in the centre of Europe.

These are the crucial points of orientation—with the proviso that no changes are made in the course of the programme.

Speech of the Federal Chancellor on October 24, 1971, at the Ordinary Meeting of the Printing and Paper Trade Union at Nuremberg (Excerpt)

In the policy towards Western Europe we have two important problems to solve: the clarification of the complicated monetary questions and the conclusion of the negotiations with the United Kingdom and the other future partners on entry to the EEC. I have just as little doubt that the British House of Commons will express its approval as I have of the ratification of the Eastern treaties by the Bundestag. When the accession of the new Member States is accomplished, the way will be clear for progress in the direction of the economic and monetary union and the development of political co-operation.

To this end I think that a summit conference of the six States of the European Community and of the four countries prepared for entry should take place in the first half of next year. It must naturally be well prepared. To this end also the Foreign Ministers will be meeting in Rome in November.

What is worrying us mostly at the present are the varying opinions on monetary policy. A common European line should be found as quickly as possible, since only then will it be possible to exert a positive influence within the larger international framework and achieve an objective balancing of interests with the United States.

In the case of the internal development of the Community, increasing importance is attached to the strengthening of the social components. I know myself to be in agreement with the trade unions that not only with us have we to realize the democratic and social Federal State, but that we must also try to achieve a better social balance within the European framework.

Interview of the Federal Chancellor for the "Report from Bonn" with German Television on October 29, 1971 (Excerpt)

Question:

Mr. Chancellor, it is said that through the entry of the United Kingdom the European development has received an incentive that will change the face of the EEC and Europe. What changes do you expect, do you hope for?

Answer:

There is, of course, no change in quality, since the British Government has accepted the Treaties of Rome and also what, on the strength of the Treaties, has developed in the meantime. In the first place it is the geographic enlargement, the quantitative enlargement, that will be stronger when Denmark, Ireland and Norway are added. The market will be larger. But, numbers apart, this enlarged Community will also receive a considerable amount of—let us say—experience in international politics, associated with the United Kingdom, and we are also acquiring something more of democratic substance. Nor would I wish to overlook technology. The United Kingdom has been meeting with all sorts of economic difficulties in recent years, but she is a highly developed—also a technologically highly developed—country.

Question:

There is the fear that the EEC might actually lose in striking power, in compactness, through Britain's entry, that it might become more an economic zone instead of advancing in the direction of a union of the European States. Do you believe this?

Answer:

No; I would prefer to put it like this. The differences of opinion about this subject will not be greater through the entry of the United Kingdom. Among the Six we have seen that the original conception of the supranational, the cosmopolitical, cannot—or only very conditionally—be realized. In the economic sphere there are powerful elements that are characterized by the supersession of the nation-State sovereignty by Community arrangements. As I see it, the difficulty is purely practical. A Council of Ministers composed of the representatives of ten States operates more awkwardly than one composed of the representatives of six. But its evolution towards a uniform whole is not handicapped; it takes place anyhow only—and even without Britain only—if it is assumed that the economic integration is accompanied by political co-operation that does not abolish the responsibility of the national Governments.

Question:

You said just now that Britain's accession to the EEC brings added international political experience. Can this Europe still play any role at all in international politics between the two great nuclear powers, the United States and the Soviet Union—which are both also factors in the policy towards Germany and towards Europe?

Answer:

I proceed on the assumption—I have always proceeded on the assumption—that Western Europe must maintain relations in the nature of a partnership as close as possible with the United States, and not merely for security policy reasons. But I am very convinced that, precisely against the background of whatever is happening in the world, Western Europe has the possibility, and the power, to exercise an influence, and not as what used to be called the "third power". What, in any case, does the "third" means? Nowadays, one talks about the triangle—also in a somewhat simplified fashion—Washington, Moscow, Pekin. Japan is also a corner of a structure of this nature. And Western Europe will also be so, not by placing itself against America but by trying, in the closest possible co-operation with America, to play its own role. And that means also playing its role in the process of achieving détente.

Statement of the Federal Chancellor on the Voting in the British House of Commons on October 28, 1971, on the United Kingdom's Accession to the EEC

I am glad there has been a majority vote in the British House of Commons in favour of Britain's entry into the European Community.

The new development will be of benefit to the British nation, as to the whole of Europe. Particularly economically, but also politically, Western Europe will be more cohesive and stronger.

I do not hesitate to ascribe historic importance to the House of Commons' decision. It should, in my opinion, have come earlier, but there is little point in arguing about the omissions of former years.

Of course my standpoint, which can surprise no one, means no interference in the conflict of opinions in which Britain finds herself at present. It is perfectly understandable that there are many people who, for reasons of tradition or on the basis of other motives, do not, or not yet, concur in the decision that has been taken. I am, however, certain that, in the course of the further development, those who have not been able to give an affirmative vote today will also become convinced of the great opportunities the Community presents.

Statement of the Federal Minister for Foreign Affairs, Walter Scheel, on the Voting in the British House of Commons on October 28, 1971

We have noted with great satisfaction the result of the voting in the British House of Commons. With this decision on principle on entry, and with the approval of the results of the negotiations to date, an important milestone has been reached on Britain's long road into the European Community. The end of this road, which started ten years ago with the first application for entry, can be foretold. There are still a few points (fishing, EFTA mandate) to be settled in the Brussels negotiations with the United Kingdom, Ireland, Denmark and Norway. The operations involved in the drafting of the Treaty of Accession are in full swing and will be concluded towards the end of the year so that the full text of the documents covering the Treaty will be to hand at the beginning of next year in the six original Member States and in the four acceding countries for the procedure to secure national assent.

It is the firm hope of the Federal Government that the decision of the British House of Commons and the attention paid it by the other candidate countries will facilitate the work that still remains to be done.

Through the decision of the British House of Commons, the Federal Government sees the confirmation of its policy, which was directed towards the enlargement of the European Communities. It was right that at the summit conference at The Hague on December 1 and 2,

1969, the representatives of the Six decided to engage in further negotiations with the United Kingdom, Ireland, Denmark and Norway. They did so in order to take into account the great political objective, to—as the communiqué says—pioneer the way to a united Europe able to assume its responsibility in the world of tomorrow and make the contribution that is appropriate to its tradition and its mission. The vehement and lengthy argumentation that preceded the voting in the House of Commons shows that the United Kingdom is conscious of the historic importance of this decision and has earnestly struggled for it.

All concerned have contributed towards the successful course of the negotiations on entry. It was possible to reach agreements in all questions dealt with because everyone was prepared, in the interest of the enlargement of the Common Market and the strengthening of Europe, to make concessions. Although at times the negotiations were not easy, they were always conducted in a businesslike and happy atmosphere. To their outcome the German side rendered a not inconsiderable contribution.

The Federal Government looks forward with firm confidence to the start of the year 1973, in which ten European States will address themselves to the great task of urging forward the internal development of the Community and consolidating its position in the world.

Statement of the Federal Government on the Decisions of the EEC and NATO at the Session of the German Bundestag on October 15, 1971 (Excerpt)

Last week produced a large number of results of political negotiations and discussions which the Federal Government considers worth reporting about to this Honourable House. You

are very conversant with the picture; the international bodies were working at high pressure to bring the long-prepared projects to a successful conclusion before Christmas.

December 11 and 12 brought us another step forward in the development of the European Economic Community. After a session lasting almost 24 hours, it was possible to reach agreement on the last of the unresolved problems—the question of fishing—with three of the countries that are prepared to enter the Community—the United Kingdom, Ireland and Denmark.

What were the actual points at issue in the negotiations of recent weeks? After the four candidate countries—all large fishing nations—had intimated their acceptance, for all practical purposes, of the EEC's fish marketing regulations, they all wished for their offshore fishing to be protected for as long a period as possible. It proved possible to agree on an arrangement which can be described as a fair compromise. The principle of the transitional arrangement was recognized, but the periods of transition were very protracted and took account of special problem areas along the candidate countries' coasts.

Only through concessions on both sides was the outcome of the negotiations reached. It demonstrates that although the Community is aware that account has to be taken of the vital interests of these countries, the countries for their part have acknowledged the basic rights of the Community.

I have already mentioned that it was only three countries with which it was possible finally to reach agreement on the last difficult problem. As expected, Norway did not concur in this solution. Because of her special circumstances, she is urging that consideration be given to a permanent exceptional arrangement for certain areas. She has, however, agreed to allow this arrangement to be subject to the possibility of revision. The difficulty now is that the other three countries are refusing to agree to an arrangement that allows Norway more latitude than they can claim for themselves. Under certain circumstances, the Community would already have been prepared to come to meet Norway a step nearer, but only if this step was restricted solely to Norway's special case.

In this situation there was nothing for it but for the time being to adhere to the agreement reached with the United Kingdom, Ireland and Denmark. We shall, therefore, have to find a solution to the problem of Norway in further negotiations. In the coming weeks, it will not be easy, in the negotiations with Norway, on the one hand to find a formula which meets Norway's requirements—which are recognized as justifiable—and, on the other, for the other three candidate countries to take this on sufferance without jeopardizing the results of the negotiations reached with them.

Whether it will be possible to achieve this by the middle of January cannot be foreseen at the moment: January, in the view of all concerned, is to be the time for the signing of the Treaty of Accession. We shall endeavour to find a solution making it possible for all four countries prepared to accede to sign the Treaty simultaneously. Should the negotiations with Norway prove too complicated, then it will be necessary to accept the fact that Norway will have to sign the Treaty on Accession at a later date.

Immediately after the signing, the Federal Government will initiate the ratification procedure, not merely to ensure that accession can become a reality on January 1, 1973, but also to demonstrate to the partners the importance that is attached to this Treaty.

A few weeks prior to the opening of the negotiations on entry, I stated on June 17, in the foreign policy debate on the policy towards Germany, Eastern Europe and Western Europe:

From the very beginning, this Federal Government has seen an urgent task in European integration and has left no doubt that progress along this road is also a prerequisite for an active policy towards our Eastern neighbours.

These pronouncements still apply. At the end of this year it can be said that the negotiations on entry have brought within reach the objective laid down at the summit conference at The Hague—namely, to help the Community to acquire the dimensions that increasingly meet the requirements of the second half of the 20th century.

Now the frame is set within which this European Community can develop in accordance with the political will of its members. Thus is created the foundation which is necessary for a long-term policy of overcoming the confrontations and bringing about, step by step, co-operation throughout Europe. We are conscious of the heavy responsibility the Federal Republic of Germany particularly has to bear, and I can certainly state that we have acted and taken decisions in accordance with our responsibility.

You will also recall that, during the last conference of the Foreign Ministers of the Ten States in Rome, I pointed out with great insistence what an endangerment to cohesion in the Western Alliance the international monetary difficulties could signify. We must do everything we possibly can together to find a solution in order to prevent the monetary questions and the increasing difficulties in the spheres of world trade resulting in disintegrating elements.

It is possible to make use of the opportunity to continue the policy of détente in Europe successfully in the near future and to arrive at more co-operation between Western and Eastern Europe only if an increasing degree of integration can be achieved in our Western alliances.

At the meeting of the Council of Ministers, the Foreign Ministers therefore dealt also with the question as to how the next meeting of the Ten in Washington, due to take place on December 17 and 18, can be made easier through appropriate decisions. At the meeting of the Ten in Rome it was seen that, in the negotiations on a worldwide realignment, the United States attaches a special role to problems of commercial policy in relation to the European Community. After, in Rome, the EEC's Ministers of Finance had indicated that the Community would be prepared to engage in negotiations on trade, the United States, through her plenipotentiary, Mr. Eberle, last week gave notice of demands which were in part very far-reaching. I myself think that it is idle to start quarrelling about the justification of American demands before any discussion whatever has begun between the European Economic Community and the United States.

The Federal Government has, therefore, consistently urged at the Council of Ministers' meetings that the Commission should authorize negotiations with the United States as soon as possible so that at last it is possible to enter into discussions. Already at the Rome meeting the Federal Government had suggested embarking on an institutionalized dialogue with North America at an early date.

You know that in this matter the EEC Member States have varying interests, and we have to put up with this situation. We have, however, fortunately succeeded in the Council of Ministers in taking a decision that envisages an early assumption of discussions. It would be desirable if the Council of the Permanent Representatives, which was commissioned with the drawing-up of a mandate for the Commission, could conclude its operations so quickly that the Commission could announce its readiness to negotiate before the 17th—18th.

Interview of the Federal Chancellor
with a dpa Correspondent in Sarasota, U.S.A., on January 7, 1972

Question:

Just like President Pompidou and Prime Minister Heath, you advocate a European summit conference, which can doubtless be reckoned with for the middle of this year. What ideas have you got on concrete steps towards an economic and monetary union within the enlarged EEC?

Answer:

So far as the date is concerned, I think it will probably be in the autumn ... So far as the development towards the economic and monetary union is concerned, I assume that the Ten—let us say it will be Ten; that is, that apart from the United Kingdom the other three also finally decide on entry—will undertake to realize in the main what was laid down in the so-called Werner Plan at the beginning of last year. This is the Plan that was named after the Prime Minister of Luxembourg and that envisages stages in the course of which the monetary union would be achieved within a decade, and

thus virtually from the '70s to the '80s. There can be modification of this when reconsidered by Ten, but I am assuming that the phased plan, which has never been cancelled and which was retarded in its initial stage only by the international monetary crisis, will be implemented by the enlarged Community. It has never been placed on ice, since, even, for instance, in these months of the difficult international monetary crisis, the discussions on the coordination and harmonization of economic policy within the existing Community have continued. The candidates for entry have already stated—it was part of the negotiations on their accession—that they will co-operate in developing the Community in the direction of the economic and monetary union. Nevertheless, so far as the working-out in practice is concerned, this will certainly be one of the main points in a summit conference of the Ten. A second main point will be the possible, increased co-operation in foreign policy within this enlarged Western European framework.

V. Chronology

The Enlargement of the European Communities. The Most Important Data on the Road to European Integration from the Summit Conference at The Hague to the Signing of the Treaties of Accession

December 1–2, 1969

Summit conference of the Heads of State and Government of the six EEC States at The Hague. The final communiqué confirms the will of the Community to enter into the final phase and to develop the Community further through the gradual creation of an economic and monetary union. It is agreed that the EEC shall have its own revenues at its disposal. There is confirmation of the political objective of the Community and the principle of the enlargement of the European Community by States prepared to accede. Agreement is reached on the initiation of negotiations on accession. Progress in political unification "in the perspective of the enlargement" is sought, and the Foreign Ministers are commissioned with the submission of an appropriate report.

December 8–9, 1969

In Brussels, the Council of the European Community lays down the modalities of the negotiations with the States prepared to accede and draws up a list of the points that have to be covered by the necessary preparations so that a common attitude is established with regard to the effective initiation of the negotiations. The Council also decides that in the final phase of the Common Market the Community can pursue a common or largely coordinated commercial policy, in which connection, exceptions according to which the Member States may, in exceptional cases, conclude bilateral agreements up to December 31, 1972, are to hold good.

December 22, 1969

The main features of the Communal Fiscal Constitution are agreed by the Council of the European Community.

December 31, 1969

Termination of the period of transition, pursuant to the Resolution of the summit conference at The Hague. Commencement of the final phase of the EEC.

January 1, 1970

From January 1, 1970, within the framework of the implementation of the Council's Ordinance of 1968 on the freedom of movement of employees in the Community, employees from the Member States no longer need permission to undertake employment in the Federal Republic.

February 5–7, 1970

On the strength of the decisions on principle of December 22, 1969, the council of the European Community, in preparation of the negotiations on accession, adopts Resolutions on the financing of the common agricultural policy, funds of its own, the budgetary procedure, and the strengthening of the powers of the European Parliament.

March 6, 1970

The drawing-up of a report on the fundamental ideas for the gradual constitution of an economic and monetary union, pursuant to the task set at the summit conference at The Hague, is handed over to an ad hoc working group following a Resolution of the Council of the European Community. This so-called Werner Group is to submit an appropriate report to the Council. For consideration, a German, a Belgian and a Luxembourg draft of a phased plan had already been submitted.

April 20–21, 1970

Resolution of the Council of the European Community on the supersession of the financial contributions of the Member States by the Communities' own revenues. Accordingly, on April 22, 1970, the representatives of the European Community States sign the Treaty on the Adjustments to Certain Budgetary Provisions of the Treaties establishing the European Communities (ECSC, EEC and EURATOM) and of the Treaty on the Institution of a Single Council and a Single Commission of the European Communities of April 4, 1965. To offset the growing fiscal autonomy of the European Community, the budgetary powers of the European Parliament are also extended by this Treaty of April 22, 1970. Agreement is reached at the same time on wine marketing regulations.

May 29, 1970

In Viterbo, near Rome, the Foreign Ministers of the Community nominate the members of the Commission, reduced from 14 to 9. On the German side, the members include Wilhelm Haferkamp as Vice-President and Ralf Dahrendorf as member. The Ministers also discuss political co-operation and decide to meet twice a year for consultations on foreign policy.

June 8–9, 1970

The preparations for the negotiations on accession are concluded. The negotiations are to commence on June 30, 1970. The Council of the European Community also approves the interim report on the gradual establishment of an economic and monetary union.

June 30, 1970

Ceremonious opening of the "Conference of the European Communities with the States which have Applied for Entry to these Communities" (Denmark, the United Kingdom, Ireland and Norway) in Luxembourg.

July 1, 1970

In his turn, Federal Minister for Foreign Affairs Walter Scheel takes over for six months

the Chair in the General Council of the European Community.

July 2, 1970

The new Commission of the European Community takes up office.

July 22, 1970

Under German chairmanship, the Council of the European Community's first separate negotiations with the United Kingdom take place. Agreement is reached on the subjects for discussion at the next negotiations and on the negotiation procedure.

September 7, 1970

As officiating President of the Council, the Federal Minister for Foreign Affairs, Walter Scheel, hands over in Bonn to the representatives of Denmark, the United Kingdom, Ireland and Norway the report on matters to do with political unification drawn up by the Foreign Ministers of the Six on the strength of the Resolutions of the Hague.

September 17, 1970

Opening of the negotiations between the Community and Japan on a trading agreement.

September 21, 1970

Initiation of the negotiations with Ireland on matters connected with accession to the European Community.

September 22–23, 1970

Initiation of the negotiations with Denmark and Norway on matters connected with accession to the European Community.

October 27, 1970

The "Report of the Foreign Ministers to the Heads of State and Government of the Member States of the European Communities on political co-operation", drawn up in accordance with Point No. 15 of the communiqué of The

Hague, is approved by the Council of the European Community and published on October 30, 1970, by the Governments of the Member States. In accordance with this Report (the so-called Davignon Report), the Foreign Ministers of the Six will meet every six months for consultations on foreign policy, to be followed by a complementary exchange of views with the Foreign Ministers of the four countries prepared to accede. A Committee composed of the Directors on the Political Departments in the Foreign Ministries is set up, its function being to prepare for these meetings.

November 10, 1970

In Brussels, the three neutral States Austria, Sweden and Switzerland notify the European Community of their wish to participate in the Common Market, at the same time preserving their neutrality.

November 19, 1970

Under the chairmanship of the Federal Minister for Foreign Affairs, the first consultations of the Foreign Ministers of the six European Community States on foreign policy take place in Munich. They agree, among other things, on a harmonized diplomatic approach to Third Countries and in international organizations and on a multilateral co-operation of the Foreign Ministries. With this is set in motion a consultation mechanism which is also to harmonize the foreign policy of the six countries in international political issues not immediately concerning them.

November 24, 1970

First negotiations between the Community and the EFTA countries not seeking entry–Iceland, Finland and Portugal.

November 25, 1970

Negotiations with Austria on an interim agreement on the mutual lowering of customs duties.

November 26, 1970

The Resolution of the reform of the European Social Fund, already approved in principle in July, 1970, is finally adopted by the Council of the European Community. The new Social Fund is to become a new dynamic instrument for the European employment policy and for taking preventive measures. On the strength of German proposals for the institution of a European social budget, the Commission of the European Community is commissioned by the Council with the submission of comparative studies and a working plan.

December 2, 1970

In Brussels, first exchange of political opinions between the Foreign Ministers of the Six and the four countries prepared to accede, with a discussion of political problems touched on at the meeting of the Foreign Ministers on November 19, 1970, in Munich.

December 5, 1970

In Valletta, an association agreement on the gradual constitution of a customs union is signed between the European Community and Malta.

February 8–9, 1971

Following the preparatory work done by the Werner Group, the Council of the European Community approves a phased plan (formal adoption on March 22, 1971) in accordance with which, retroactive from January 1, 1971, the Community is to be developed in three stages from a customs union into an economic and monetary union within the next ten years. (A "prudence clause", approved following the German proposal, is to serve the compulsory parallel development of an economic and a monetary union.) Decisions are also taken on the strengthening of co-operation between the central banks, the strengthening of the coordination of the short-term economic policy, and the introduction of a mechanism for medium-term financial assistance.

March 9, 1971

Walter Behrend (SPD) is elected President of the European Parliament.

March 30, 1971

The Council of the European Community decides to introduce general customs preferences for the developing countries on July 1, 1971, in deviation for the first time from the principle of the most favoured nation in order to promote the industrial development, the economic growth and the trade of the developing countries. First of all, some 91 developing countries benefit from this measure.

April 26–27, 1971

At their meeting in Hamburg, the Economics and Finance Ministers of the European Community fail to agree on joint action in the monetary question.

May 8–9, 1971

After difficult negotiations, the Council of the Economic Community agrees on a compromise for the averting of negative consequences the crisis in the international monetary system has had on, particularly, the D-Mark. With the approval of the Council, flexible rates of exchange are introduced on a temporary basis in the Federal Republic and the Netherlands.

May 11–12, 1971

The European Ministers of Agriculture agree on offset levies in favour of the Federal Republic and the Netherlands to avert losses in revenue by agriculture as a result of the decisions on currency.

May 13–14, 1971 and May 18, 1971

Under French chairmanship, the second consultation meeting in accordance with the Council's decision of October 27, 1970, be-

tween the six Foreign Ministers of the European Community countries takes place in Paris. The discussion centres mainly on certain problems connected with a conference on security and co-operation in Europe affecting the Community countries and the Middle East question. In Paris, the exchange of views between the six Foreign Ministers and those of the four countries prepared to accede takes place.

June 3, 1971

For the first time the Council of the European Community meets at the level of the Ministers of Justice in Luxembourg.

June 15, 1971

At their meeting in Luxembourg, the Ministers of Economics and Finance discuss the international monetary problems, the possibilities of a return to firm parities within the Economic Community, and the stoppage of exceptional inflows of capital. They approve a Memorandum submitted by the Commission of the European Community on the market prospects in the Community and adopt as their own the conclusions contained therein on the desirable short-term economic policy.

June 22, 1971

Scarcely a year after the opening of the negotiations on accession, it is possible, in Luxembourg, to achieve agreement between the European Community and the United Kingdom on almost all important questions affecting entry.
Parallel to the negotiations with the United Kingdom, large agreement is also reached with Ireland and Denmark. Agreement in certain important points is also reached with Norway.

July 26, 1971

Agreement is reached in the Council of the European Community that in the period between the conclusion of the negotiations and the entering of the Treaties of Accession into force, the candidates will be informed and consulted in important questions also of interest to countries seeking entry as soon as the Community has itself developed guiding principles of its own.

August 19, 1971

On the strength of the American decisions on economic and monetary policy of August 15, 1971, the Council of the European Community discusses the position although it is unable to agree on the proposals for a crash programme put forward by the German delegation and the Benelux countries. It recognizes the need for a reform of the international monetary system, and particularly for the re-fixing of exchange rate parities, and announces its intention to try to secure a common attitude in the internationally competent bodies.

August 20, 1971

For the first time, the Community draws the four candidate countries into consultations in the monetary crisis. Following this, on August 20 a close co-operation and consultations in all monetary questions is also agreed for the future between the European Community and the candidates.

September 13, 1971

The Council of the European Council agrees on common principles for the reform of the world monetary system that has now become indispensable (realignment of the currency parities, including the dollar, greater flexibility towards the outside, development of the special drawing rights, demand for the abolition of the United States import levies). With this, the community is placed in the position of being able to preserve a common front in important international discussions.

October 15–16, 1971

On the strength of the proposals of the Commission for the reform of the common agricultural policy (Mansholt Plan), the Council commissions the European Community's Ministers of Agriculture with the submission of a list of the national standpoints ot the special Agricultural Committee and the Permanent Representatives.

October 28, 1971

The British House of Commons, by a majority of 112 votes, and the British House of Lords, by a majority of 451 votes to 58, vote for the entry of the United Kingdom into the European Community.

November 5–6, 1971

In Bracciono, near Rome, the Foreign Ministers of the six European Community countries meet for their third consultation conference under Italian chairmanship. They exchange views on, among other things, relations with the Middle East and the preparation of a conference on security and co-operation in Europe. They advocate a summit conference in 1972.

There follows in Rome the exchange of views between the six Foreign Ministers and the four countries prepared to accede at which it is decided that all ten countries shall participate in the planned summit conference and shall also make joint preparations for it.

November 8, 1971

After discussions with the EFTA countries not seeking entry had already a long time ago started on their relationship with the EEC, the Foreign Ministers, at their Council meeting in Brussels, issued a mandate to the Commission for the negotiation of a free trade agreement with these States (Sweden, Iceland, Switzerland, Austria, Portugal, Finland).

November 9, 1971

In Vienna, the Commission of the European Community starts the negotiations with the International Atomic Energy Organization

(IAEO) on an agreement on the verification of the control stipulations of the non-proliferation of atomic weapons treaty.

November 16, 1971

In Brussels, agreement is reached at the first Council meeting of the Ministers competent for educational matters in the European Community on the establishment of a "European University Institute", to be located in Florence.

November 30–December 1, 1971

The group of the ten important industrial countries meets in Rome (with the participation also of Switzerland).

December 18, 1971

In Washington, the Economics and Finance Ministers of the "Ten" agree on:

● a general realignment that includes a raising of the price of gold and lays down rates to govern all other currencies of the countries concerned,

● an extension of the band widths to a total of 4.5 per cent.,

● the listing of the American extra duty on imports and

● the initiation of discussions on commercial policy between the EEC and Japan on the one hand and the United States on the other.

January 14, 1972

Conclusion of the negotiations with Denmark on entry.

January 14, 1972

Negotiations between the European Community and the United States on commercial policy reliefs in connection with the decisions taken by the "Ten" on December 18, 1971.

January 17–19, 1972

Conclusion of the negotiations with the United Kingdom, Ireland and Norway on entry.

January 22, 1972

In a happy atmosphere, signing of the Treaties of Accession in Brussels.

VI. The Enlarged Community in Figures

The following Tables comprise a compilation of figures important for the Community. They cannot provide a complete statistical picture of the Community; nor is this their task. They do, however, give a glimpse of the ratios of size, in comparison also with the United States, the Soviet Union and Japan.

The figures were compiled by the Statistical Office of the European Communities from their own sources and from sources of the OECD and the United Nations.

Signs and abbreviations used:

–	nothing
.	no verification available
( )	uncertain or doubtful particulars
$	dollar
kg	kilogramme
km	kilometre
lbs.	pounds
SKE	hard coal unit = the amount of heat given by 7,000 kilo-calories

kw-hr	kilowatt hours (Board of Trade units)
GWh	Gigawatt hours $= 10^6$ kilowatt hours
EEC	European Economic Community
EFTA	European Free Trade Association

Gross National Product (GNP) at market prices: The GNP is the value of all goods and services that are consumed, invested or exported in a national product in a particular period (1 year) and that (as a rule) possess a market value reduced by that of imports. The GNP is the basis most used for estimating the productive power of a national economy.

Volume index: or *Production index*, shows, in contrast to the price index, actual changes within a certain space of time and thus eliminating the rises in price that have occurred in the meantime. These indices are not calculated at the prices ruling at the time (the current prices) but at the constant prices (e.g., the 1963 basis).

Table 1 Survey (1970)

	Six	Ten	United States	Soviet Union	Japan
Population (in 1,000s)	189,787	257,242	205,395	244,000	103,540
GNP (in $1,000 mill.)	485.2	637.4	933.3	288	
Imports as a whole (% world as a whole)					
incl. "intra-trade"	*30.3*	*41.0*	*13.7*	*4.0*	*6.5*
excl. "intra-trade"	*18.3*	*25.8*	*16.0*	*4.7*	*7.6*
Exports as a whole (% world as a whole)					
incl. "intra-trade"	*31.8*	*41.2*	*15.5*	*4.6*	*6.9*
excl. "intra-trade"	*19.2*	*25.2*	*18.4*	*5.2*	*8.2*
Total domestic consumption of primary energy–mill. tons HCU	845.8	1,235.8	2,250.6		379.6
Production of crude steel (in 1,000 tons)	109,191	138,943	122,120	116,000	93,322
Production of motor vehicles (passenger and estate cars–in 1,000s)	8,029,000	9,670,000	6,550,000	348,000	3,179,000
Consumption of power and steel per inhabitant for industrial purposes, in kw-hr	1,672	1,736	[3,300]	[1,896]	[1,860]
Other purposes, in kw-hr	1,070	1,387	[4,000]	[698]	[1,228]
No. of motor vehicles on Jan. 1, 1971	41,827	56,009	89,861	[1,700]	8,779
Passenger cars (in 1,000s) per inhabitant	220	218	432	7	85
Television sets (in 1,000s)	40,038	58,300	81,000	30,744	21,879
per 1,000 inhabitants	216	231	399	127	214
Telephones (in 1,000s)	34,255	51,297	115,222	12,000	19,899
per 1,000 inhabitants	185	203	567	50	194

Table 2   Area and population

Area, population and no. of inhabitants per sq. km. (sq. mile) in 1970–Population forecasts

	Area 1,000 sq. kms.	Population (in 1,000s)	Inhabitants per sq. km.	Forecast of population development (in 1,000s) 1975	1980
Germany	248.5	61,508	248	62,140	63,520
France	551.2	50,770	93	52,640	54,800
Italy	301.2	54,459	181	56,490	58,410
Netherlands	33.5	13,019	356	13,660	14,460
Belgium	30.5	9,691	318	9,900	10,150
Luxembourg	2.6	340	131	(340)	(350)
Six	1,167.5	189,787	163	195,170	201,690 ´
United Kingdom	244.0	55,711	228	57,140	58,890[1])
Rep. of Ireland	68.9	2,944	42	3,120	3,330
Norway	323.9	3,879	12	4,100	4,270
Denmark	43.0	4,921	114	5,100	5,300
Ten	1,847.3	257,242	139	264,630	273,480
United States	9,363.4	205,395	22	215,600	227,500
Soviet Union	22,402.2	244,000	11	260,800	277,800
Japan	369.7	103,540	280	–	–

[1]) 1981.

Table 3   Civilians in gainful employment according to economic sectors (in 1,000s)

		Agriculture and Forestry	Industry[1])	Services[2])	Un-employed	Total
Germany	1970	2,406	13,247	11,052	149	26,854
France	1970	2,898	8,321	9,254	356	20,826
Italy	1970	3,683	8,209	6,882	615	19,389
Netherlands	1970	330	1,871	2,337	56	4,593
Belgium	1970	181	1,676	1,890	76	3,823
Luxembourg	1970	16	67	61	0	144
Six	1970	9,514	33,391	31,475	1,252	75,629
United Kingdom	1970	(715)*	(11,714)*	(12,475)	555	25.459
Rep. of Ireland	1969	301	315	445	58	1,119
Norway	1969	217	543	714	16	1,490
Denmark	1969	272	884	1,138	25	2,319
Ten		11,019*	46,847*	46,247*	1,906	106,016
United States	1969	3,606	26,253	48,043	2,831	80,733
Soviet Union	–	–	–	–	–	–
Japan	1969	9,460	17,670	23,270	570	50,980

*) Estimated.
[1]) Incl. building industry.
[2]) Incl. trade and transport.

Table 4   Gross national product at market prices (in $1,000 mill.)[1])

	1958	1970
Germany	59.2	186.4
France	53.6	147.6
Italy	30.3	93.2
Netherlands	9.5	31.3
Belgium	10.4	25.7
Luxembourg	0.4	1.0
Six	163.4	485.2
United Kingdom	64.8	121.4
Rep. of Ireland	1.4	3.8
Norway	4.0	11.4
Denmark	5.0	15.6
Ten	238.6	637.4
United States	455.0	993.3
Soviet Union	–	(288)[2])
Japan	32.0	196.2

[1]) At current prices and exchange rates.
[2]) Since the expression "gross national product" does not exist in the Soviet Union, it is easiest to use the comparable expression "net material product", which by and large represents the sum total of goods and services produced in any one year.

Table 5   Development of the gross national product at market prices (Indices of volume):
(Indices of volume): 1963 = 100

	1958	1963	1970
Germany	75.4	100	130.4
France	76.1	100	147.7
Italy	72.7	100	142.9
Netherlands	79.0	100	148.2
Belgium	79.9	100	139.2
Luxembourg	.	100	130.4
Six	75.6	100	148.9
United Kingdom	84.3	100	120.8
Rep. of Ireland	80.4	100	129.6
Norway	79.6	100	138.7
Denmark	78.1	100	141.7
Ten	77.8	100	138.2
United States	81.5	100	131.2
Soviet Union	.	100	.
Japan	59.0	100	189.4[1])

[1]) 1969.

Table 6 Average annual rates of growth of the gross national product at market prices – 1960–1970 (at constant prices)

	Total	Per inhabitant
Germany	4.8	3.7
France	5.8	4.7
Italy	5.7	4.8
Netherlands	5.1	3.8
Belgium	4.9	4.3
Luxembourg	3.4	2.6
Six	5.3	4.3
United Kingdom	2.8	2.2
Rep. of Ireland	3.9	3.5
Norway	5.0	4.2
Denmark	4.8	4.1
Ten	4.7	3.8
United States	4.0	2.7
Soviet Union	–	–
Japan	11.1	9.9

Table 7 Contributions of the economic sectors to the gross domestic product at factor costs–as percentages

	Agriculture, forestry, fishery	Industry (incl. building trades)	Services and State
	1970	1970	1970
Germany	3.8	52.3	43.9
France	.	.	.
Italy	10.3	40.5	49.3
Netherlands	6.2	42.0	51.8
Belgium	4.4	42.5	53.0
Luxembourg	4.9	55.6	39.5
Six	.	.	.
United Kingdom	3.1	44.4	52.5
Rep. of Ireland	17.8 *	35.2*	47.0*
Norway	6.3	39.9	53.7
Denmark	7.9	40.1	52.0
Ten	.	.	.
United States	2.9	35.8	61.3
Soviet Union	.	.	.
Japan	8.7	41.2	50.0

*) 1969.

Table 8 Production of selected agricultural products

	1 Grain[1]) in 1,000 tons 1968–70[2])	3 Milk in 1,000 tons 1969	4 Wine in 1,000 hectolitres 1968–70[2])	2 Meat in 1,000 tons 1969
Germany	18,414	22,262	6,245	3,858
France	32,482	31,061	58,783	4,005
Italy	14,864	10,417	70,369	1,957
Netherlands	1,541	7,975	10	1,098
Belgium	1,723	3,908	9	730
Luxembourg	137	211	120	21
Six	69,161	75,834	135,536	11,669
United Kingdom	12,269	12.764	–	2,721
Rep. of Ireland	1,415	3,678	–	592
Norway	711	1,771	–	160
Denmark	6,631	4,877	–	1,074
Ten	91,187	98,924	135,536	16,216
United States	192,966	52,707	12,413	23,227
Soviet Union	160,145	81,500	20,383	9,520
Japan	1,742	4,513	197	1,136

[1]) Excl. rice.
[2]) Average.

Table 9 Domestic consumption of primary energy and equivalents–mill. of tons HCU

	Hard and soft coal	Crude oil	Natural gas	Primary electricity	Primary energy altogether
Germany	127.9	179.6	18.4	10.2	337.2
France	51.7	130.8	12.0	19.2	214.5
Italy	12.7	115.3	15.4	16.1	160.0
Netherlands	7.3	39.6	22.4	0	69.3
Belgium	18.9	34.1	5.0	0.2	58.3
Luxembourg	3.9	2.0	0	0.8	6.7
Six	222.0	501.3	73.3	47.2	845.8
United Kingdom	155.0	140.5	14.6	10.8	320.9
Rep. of Ireland	1.3	5.8	–	0.3	7.4
Norway	1.3	11.4	–	20.0	32.7
Denmark	3.8	26.7	–	1.5	29.0
Ten	383.8	685.7	87.9	76.5	1.235.8
United States	476.0	897.1	780.1	97.4	2,250.6
Soviet Union	.	.	280.0	44.2	.
Japan	89.7	259.3	2.7	27.9	379.6

Table 10 Production of pig-iron, crude steel and rolled steel sections: 1970–in 1,000 tons

	Pig-iron	Crude steel	Rolled steel sections
Germany	33,627	45,041	31,967
France	19,128	23,774	17,825
Italy	8,354	17,277	13,180
Netherlands	3,594	5,030	3,339
Belgium	10,955	12,607	9,274
Luxembourg	4,810	5,462	3,929
Six	80,467	109,191	79,507
United Kingdom	17,671	28,329	20,668
Rep. of Ireland	–	80	70
Norway	1,249	870	427
Denmark	215	473	431
Ten	99,602	138,943	101,103
United States	83,233	122,120	79,661
Soviet Union	85,900	116,000	83,938
Japan	68,046	93,322	75,791

Table 11 Importance of foreign trade–1970

	Imports			Exports			Balance ($ mill.)
	$ mill.	% of the GNP	per inhabitant	$ mill.	% of the GNP	per inhabitant	
Germany	29,814	16.0	482	34,089	18.3	553	+4,375
France	18,922	12.8	371	17,739	12.0	348	—1,183
Italy	14,939	15.1	273	13,210	14.3	242	—1,729
Netherlands	13,393	42.9	1,021	11,767	37.7	897	—1,626
Belgium Luxembourg	11,353	42.8	1,132	11,595	43.8	1,156	+ 242
Six	88,422	18.3	464	88,499	18.3	464	+ 77
United Kingdom	21,723	18.1	390	19,351	16.2	347	—2,372
Rep. of Ireland	1,569	40.9	533	1,035	27.6	352	— 534
Norway	3,697	32.2	953	2,455	21.4	633	+1,242
Denmark	4,835	28.1	891	3,290	21.1	669	—1,095
Ten	119,795*	18.9	464	114,631*	18.0	444	—5,164
United States	33,963	4.0	195	43,226	4.4	210	+3,263
Soviet Union	11,739	.	49	12,800	.	53	+1,061
Japan	18,881	9.6	182	19,318	9.8	187	+ 437

*) These figures also include the home trade of the Ten States of the enlarged European Community.

Table 12   Development of imports as a whole–$ mill.

	1967	1968	1969	1970 $ mill.	1970 Percentage share in world imports as a whole
Germany	17,351	20,150	24,926	29,814	10.2
France	12,377	13,927	17,222	18,922	6.5
Italy	9,827	10,286	12,467	14,939	5.1
Netherlands	8,337	9,293	10,991	13,393	4.6
Belgium Luxembourg	7,176	8,333	9,989	11,353	3.9
Six	55,068	61,988	75,594	88,422	30.3
United Kingdom	17,714	18,959	19,956	21,723	7.4
Rep. of Ireland	1,077	1,175	1,413	1,569	0.5
Norway	2,746	2,706	2,943	3,697	1.3
Denmark	3,134	3,213	3,800	4,385	1.5
Ten	79,739	88,042	103,706	119,795	41.0
United States	26,732	32,992	36,052	39,963	13.7
Soviet Union	9,220	9,410	10,327	11,739	4.0
Japan	11,663	12,987	15,024	18,881	6.5

Table 13   Development of exports as a whole–$ mill.

	1967	1968	1969	1970 $ mill.	1970 Percentage share in world exports as a whole
Germany	21,736	24,842	29,052	34,189	12.3
France	11,377	12,612	14,880	17,739	6.4
Italy	8,705	10,186	11,729	13,210	4.7
Netherlands	7,288	8,341	9,965	11,767	4.2
Belgium Luxembourg	7,032	8,164	10,065	11,595	4.2
Six	56,139	64,145	75,691	88,499	31.8
United Kingdom	14,372	15,346	16,894	19,351	6.9
Rep. of Ireland	784	798	891	1,035	0.4
Norway	1,736	1,938	2,203	2,455	0.9
Denmark	2,474	2,852	2,958	3,290	1.2
Ten	75,505	84,809	98,637	114,631	41.2
United States	31,147	33,932	37,444	43,226	15.5
Soviet Union	9,652	10,634	11,655	12,800	4.6
Japan	10,441	12,972	15,990	19,318	6.9

Table 14   Imports as a whole according to countries of origin: 1970–in $ mill.

	Imports as a whole	of which from			
		EEC	EFTA	United States	Rest of the world
Germany	29,814	13,233	4,464	5,293	8,824
France	18,922	9,256	1,980	1,896	5,790
Italy	14,939	6,146	1,588	1,543	5,662
Netherlands	13,393	7,483	1,498	1,308	3,104
Belgium Luxembourg	11,353	6,683	1,196	996	2,479
Six	88,422	42,800	10,725	9,035	25,862
United Kingdom	21,723	4,373	3,374	2,815	11,161
Rep. of Ireland	1,569	259	933	110	267
Norway	3,697	920	1,645	267	865
Denmark	4,835	1,457	1,808	327	793
Ten	119,793	49,810	18,486	12,554	38,945
United States	39,963	6,612	3,812	–	29,539
Soviet Union	11,739	1,170	619	115	9,835
Japan	18,881	1,117	762	5,564	11,438

Table 15   Imports as a whole according to countries of origin: 1970 – as percentages

	Imports as a whole	of which from			
		EEC	EFTA	United States	Rest of the world
Germany	100	44.4	15.0	11.0	29.6
France	100	48.9	10.5	10.0	30.6
Italy	100	41.2	10.6	10.3	37.9
Netherlands	100	55.9	11.2	9.7	23.2
Belgium Luxembourg	100	58.9	10.5	8.8	21.8
Six	100	48.4	12.1	10.2	29.3
United Kingdom	100	20.1	15.5	13.0	51.4
Rep. of Ireland	100	16.5	59.5	7.0	17.0
Norway	100	24.9	44.5	7.2	23.4
Denmark	100	33.2	41.2	7.5	18.1
Ten	100	41.6	15.4	10.5	32.5
United States	100	1.6	9.5	–	73.9
Soviet Union	100	10.0	5.3	1.0	83.7
Japan	100	5.9	4.0	29.5	60.6

Table 16 Exports as a whole according to countries of destination: 1970–in $ mill.

	Exports as a whole	of which to			
		EEC	EFTA	United States	Rest of the world
Germany	34,189	13,726	7,734	3,124	9,605
France	17,739	8,661	2,325	954	5,799
Italy	13,210	5,673	1,827	134	4,356
Netherlands	11,767	7,290	1,775	506	2,196
Belgium Luxembourg	11,595	7,950	1,224	696	1,725
Six	88,500	43,300	14,885	6,633	23,681
United Kingdom	19,351	4,209	3,064	2,258	9,820
Rep. of Ireland	1,035	120	700	104	111
Norway	2,455	729	1,135	141	450
Denmark	3,290	746	1,639	263	642
Ten	114,631	49,104	21,423	9,400	34,704
United States	43,226	8,423	4,506	–	30,297
Soviet Union	12,800	859	733	64	11,144
Japan	19,318	1,303	1,112	6,015	10,888

Table 17 Exports as a whole according to countries of destination: 1970–as percentages

	Exports as a whole	of which to			
		EEC	EFTA	United States	Rest of the world
Germany	100	40.2	22.6	9.1	28.1
France	100	48.8	13.1	5.4	32.7
Italy	100	42.9	13.8	10.3	33.0
Netherlands	100	61.9	15.1	4.3	18.7
Belgium Luxembourg	100	68.6	10.5	6.0	14.9
Six	100	48.9	16.8	7.5	26.8
United Kingdom	100	21.8	15.8	11.7	50.7
Rep. of Ireland	100	11.6	67.6	10.1	10.7
Norway	100	29.7	46.2	5.8	18.3
Denmark	100	22.7	49.8	8.0	19.5
Ten	100	42.8	18.7	8.2	30.3
United States	100	19.5	10.4	–	70.1
Soviet Union	100	6.7	5.7	0.5	87.1
Japan	100	6.7	5.8	31.1	56.4

Table 18 Consumption of selected foodstuffs per inhabitant and year in the 1969–70 economic year

	Grain	Meat (dead weight)	Vegetables	Fresh milk	Wine
	kilos. lbs.	kilos. lbs.	kilos. lbs.	kilos. lbs.	pints litres
Germany	66.0	73.2	65.4	77.9	16.9
France	77.9	84.5	130.8	97.2	108.2
Italy	126.6	47.8	170.1	65.2	114.9
Netherlands	64.5	51.3	80.6	113.9	4.1
Belgium					12.0
Luxembourg	79.1	67.1	87.4	80.7	37.0
Six	87.2	67.6[1])	115.1	82.0	68.1
United Kingdom	72.7	73.4[2])	62.2	143.4	.
Rep. of Ireland	92.7	81.0	60.0	213.3	.
Norway	69.0	(41.7)	33.4	175.8	.
Denmark	67.9	61.5	42.1	121.2	.
Ten	83.5	.	100.4	98.9	.
United States	61.7	100.0[2])	91.9	125.5	.
Soviet Union	156.2	38.7[3])	67.9	173.7	.
Japan	34.3	17.4[2])	120.1	24.3	. .

[1]) 1968–69.
[2]) 1969 calendar year, meat as a whole.
[3]) 1964–66.

Table 19 No. of motor vehicles–January 1, 1971

	Passenger cars in 1000s	per 1,000 inhabitants	Commercial vehicles in 1000s
Germany	14,377	234	1,192
France	12,470	245	1,900
Italy	10,209	187	929
Netherlands	2,600	200	350
Belgium	2,080	215	277
Luxembourg	91	267	13
Six	41,827	220	4,661
United Kingdom	12,000	213	1,945
Rep. of Ireland	358	122	49
Norway	747	193	152
Denmark	1,077	219	252
Ten	56,009	218	7,059
United States	89,861	432	[19,116]
Soviet Union	[1,700]	7	[4,200]
Japan	8,779	85	8,803

Table 20 Registered television sets and telephones–January 1, 1971

	Television sets		Telephones	
	in 1,000s	per 1,000 inhabitants	in 1,000s	per 1,000 inhabitans
Germany	15,970	262	12,456	212
France	10,121	201	8,114	161
Italy	9,016	170	8,528	160
Netherlands	2,869	223	3,120	242
Belgium	2,000	207	1,931	200
Luxembourg	62	183	106	311
Six	40,038	216	34,255	185
United Kingdom	15,792	284	14,061	253
Rep. of Ireland	446	153	287	98
Norway	796	207	1,091	283
Denmark	1,228	250	1,603	328
Ten	58,300	231	51,297	203
United States	81,000	399	115,222	567
Soviet Union	30,744	127	12,000	50
Japan	21,879	214	19,899	194

Table 21 Medical care–end 1969

	Doctors		Chemists		Hospital beds	
	in 1,000s	per 100,000 inhabitants	in 1,000s	per 100,000 inhabitants	in 1,000s	per 100,000 inhabitants
Germany	93.9	154.5	20.2	33	677.7	1,102
France	62.4	123.0	23.4	46	543.5	1,071
Italy	97.4	179	35.4	65	542.8[1])	997
Netherlands	16.3	125	1.1	9.5	91.1[2])	701
Belgium	14.9	154	6.5	67.7	74.5[2])	769
Luxembourg	0.4	106	0.2	50	4.3	1,265
Six	285.3	150	86.8	46	1,933.9	1,017
United Kingdom	63.1	113	16.7	30	541.3	972
Rep. of Ireland	3.0	102	1.7	58	38.5	1,308
Norway	5.4	139	0.8	21	46.0	1,186
Denmark	6.6	134	1.8	37	43.4	881
Ten	.	.	.	.	.	.
United States	338.4	165	120[2])	58	1.663	810
Soviet Union	591.9	247	45.1	19	2.567.3	1.067
Japan	116.0	112	76.1	74	1.033.6	998

[1]) 1968.
[2]) 1966.

136